Discovering Life's Directions

Discovering Life's Directions

Making Spiritually Insightful Decisions about Your Future

J. Murray Elwood

AVE MARIA PRESS Notre Dame, Indiana 46556

Permissions and Credits:

Excerpt from *The Active Life: A Spirituality of Work, Creativity, and Caring* by Parker J. Palmer, copyright © 1990 by Parker J. Palmer. Reprinted by permission of Harper Collins Publishers, Inc.

Excerpt from *An American Childhood* by Annie Dillard, copyright © 1987 by Annie Dillard. Reprinted by permission of Harper Collins Publishers, Inc.

Excerpt from "Because of the Stories," by Andrew M. Greeley, copyright © 1994 by The New York Times Company. Reprinted by permission.

Excerpt from *The Call of Service,* copyright © 1993 by Robert Coles. Reprinted by permission of Houghton Mifflin Co. All rights reserved.

Scripture quotations are from the *New Revised Standard Version Bible ,* copyright © 1993, Division of Christian Education of the National Council of Churches of Christ in the United States of America. All rights reserved.

Excerpt from *Pigeon Feathers and Other Stories* by John Updike, copyright © 1962 by Jophn Updike. Reprinted by permission of Alfred A. Knopf, Inc.

Excerpts from *The Power and The Glory* by Graham Greene, copyright © 1940, 1968 by Graham Greene. Used by permission of Viking Penguin, a division of Penguin Books, USA, Inc.

Excerpt from *Telling Secrets* by Frederick Buechner, copyright © 1991 by Frederick Buechner. Reprinted by permission of Harper Collins Publishers, Inc.

"The Road Ahead" from *Thoughts in Solitude* by Thomas Merton, copyright © 1956, 1958 by the Abbey of Our Lady of Gethsemani. Copyright © renewed in 1986 by the trustees of the Thomas Merton Legacy Trust.

Excerpt from *Two Part Invention* by Madeleine L'Engle. Copyright © 1988 by Crosswicks Ltd. Reprinted by permission of Farrar, Straus & Giroux, Inc.

Excerpt from *When the Hearts Waits* by Sue Monk Kidd, copyright © 1990 by Sue Monk Kidd. Reprinted by permission of HarperCollins Publishers, Inc.

Excerpts from *Working Ourselves to Death* by Diane Fassel, copyright © 1990 by Diane Fassel. Reprinted by permission of Harper Collins Publishers, Inc.

International Standard Book Number: 0-87793-561-0

Library of Congress Catalog Card Number: 95-78701

Cover and text design by Elizabeth J. French

Printed and bound in the United States of America.

For Sylvia,
who has shared my journey,
Ζώη μοῦ, σᾶς ἀγαπῶ

Acknowledgements

Many people have assisted me in writing this book, but I owe a particular word of thanks to a special few who, by their contributions or encouraging words, have nurtured the creative process: Edward J. O'Heron, Joanne and Mark Carroll, Susan Ryan, John T. McGraw, Amy Withington, Ed Doyle, Sister Mary Peter, and the many participants of my spiritual journey workshops who so generously shared their "search for God in story and time." Frank Cunningham, who has been my literary counselor for more years than we both like to remember, is a good friend, an editor of great sensitivity and, for me, a wonderfully challenging and knowing mentor. I thank him, and especially my wife, Sylvia, for their never-failing encouragement and inspiration.

STRAFFORD, FEBRUARY 1995

Contents

INTRODUCTION

Seeking God in Time and Story

READING SIGNS

Peggy Noonan, the former presidential speech writer, describes in her book *Life, Liberty and the Pursuit of Happiness*, a time in her life when she was at a personal crossroads. She called an acquaintance, a resigned Jesuit priest, and described for him her spiritual "symptoms." She was experiencing something like a hunger, Noonan told this friend, a desire, a thirst for things of the spirit. Her friend listened, read the signs, and replied, "That's the language of conversion."

Discovering Life's Directions is a book about reading those kinds of signs—recognizing and then interpreting the events and moments in our lives that help us identify our directions. A career management consultant, getting to know a new client, for example, will ask that person to describe past crossroads, significant choices, in his or her life. The consultant isn't interested so much in the *facts* of the person's life, but is listening for the *process*, the way the client chooses, the criteria used, the factors that enter into his or her decision-making.

I am a lawyer with graduate degrees in psychology and religious studies. For several years, both as a law school administrator and in private practice, I have worked as a career management consultant, with lawyers and other professionals "in transition"—men and women devastated by an unanticipated termination or just burnt out in their careers and seeking healing as well as new directions. I have noticed that behind much of the bravado and many of the problems they describe, such as compulsive perfectionism, work addiction, and fractured relationships, is often a profound emptiness of spirit. And I have seen those signs in religious professionals as much as I have detected them in corporate executives.

I also offer a program on discernment that has been received enthusiastically at a Catholic college and as part of the adult education program of a nearby monastery. I have counseled friends seeking new personal and professional paths. And I have gone through several career crises myself. I'm writing this book to share some of my own experience and insights. I don't give instant answers, but I do try to provide a different perspective and involve those with whom I work in a discerning process. This approach has helped other men and women define and then identify their directions, and I believe it will prove valuable to you.

So, in the chapters that follow, I am going to act as your personal career consultant, spiritual guide, and coach. I will help you review, through a variety of exercises, significant transitional events in your human journey. More important, I will also insist that you reflect prayerfully on the meaning of these moments in your spiritual sojourn, first in your childhood, then adolescence, and finally, adult life.

Taking time to reflect on the story of our lives—and on the stories *in* our lives—is important. As scripture clearly demonstrates, there are moments when the Lord intervenes in our lives, but we do not recognize him; we become aware of his presence only later, after his departure. Thus Jacob, after his vision, cries out: "Surely the Lord is in this place—and I did not know it!" (Gn 28:16). Gideon also understood the meaning of his visitation later, after the angel had departed and said, "Help me, Lord God! For I have seen the angel of the Lord face to face" (Jgs 6:22). Even Peter, while being freed from prison, had "no clear realization that this was taking place through the angel's help. The whole thing seemed to him a mirage." Only later, after he had escaped from prison, he "came to himself . . . and said, 'Now I am sure that the Lord has sent his angel to rescue me'" (Acts 12:9-11).

Many of us, as we begin to review our life's story, have had an experience similar to those of these biblical personages. Our God is a God of surprises, revealed to us in new and unexpected ways. We listen to our life as a whole for whatever we may be able to hear of meaning, of holiness, of God. We discover that God has "spoken" to us, too, at sundry times and in diverse manners, either at special moments of our lives or through our religious traditions and institutions, and we neither knew it nor recognized the Lord's presence at the time.

We are like Emily in Thornton Wilder's play *Our Town*. Emily was a young wife and mother who died in childbirth; she comes back for a moment to her hometown, Grover's Corners, to see herself again as she was on the day of her twelfth birthday. The vision is almost too terrible to bear, because she suddenly realizes the beauty and depth of the commonplace, taken-for-granted moments of her life—things like clocks ticking, her mother's sunflowers, food and coffee, newly-ironed dresses and hot baths, sleeping and waking up. In her anguish, she cries out, "Oh, earth, you're too wonderful for anybody to realize you. Do any human beings ever realize life while they live it?—every, every minute?"

EXPECTATIONS

For several years now I have listened to the stories of many different career changers, shared their journeys, and I consider myself skilled in the art of career counseling. For over twenty years I was also a spiritual guide for men and women from all walks of life, both lay and religious professionals. In addition to my graduate degree in religious studies, my special area of expertise is the spiritual teaching of John Henry Newman, that great nineteenth-century religious guide, Oxford scholar, Anglican clergyman, and later, Catholic cardinal. I have read almost all of Newman's sermons, a large number of his letters offering spiritual direction, and am the author of *Kindly Light*, a book on his spiritual teaching.

Another contemporary spiritual writer, Thomas Moore, introduces his book *Care of the Soul* by reminding his readers that what he writes is really a parody, a "fiction," of self-help books, because "no one can tell you how to live your life. No one knows the secrets of the heart sufficiently to tell others about them authoritatively." I couldn't agree more.

I point out to every new client within five minutes of our first meeting that nobody can live others' lives for them; no one dare take responsibility for another person's life. Nobody can gesture in one direction or another and say, "Here is the way you are to go; this is the path you must follow." But some people never hear me. Sure, they nod their heads and smile and say they understand, but they don't really hear. They talk, and I listen. Then, sooner or later, they look me in the eye and plead, "But what do you really think I should do?"

People desperately want directions, but they fear personal accountability. So they search for the perfect book, the most sensitive counselor, or the latest media guru, someone who will tell them exactly what they are to do with their lives. And when, after a time, they aren't satisfied with the answers they have received, they move on to the next new book, trade in one spiritual guide for a newer model, and continue their restless search, never really *discerning* their new directions.

These career changers and chronic drifters, moving relentlessly from one source of advice to another, are little different from the corporate lawyer I once knew who spent six precious weeks following his "termination" tinkering with ten different versions of his resume. A marketing executive wasted the first two months of her job search drafting three-page personalized replies to *Wall Street Journal* ads and designing forms to track her not-yet-started networking campaign. Both obsessive tinkerers and spiritual drifters need to be reminded that motion is not the same as movement, and activity is not necessarily action.

A PROCESS, NOT A PRODUCT

Early into our first meeting I make sure my clients understand this: A career decision is not something for purchase, like a new car, or a computer, or suit of clothes. It is, rather, a dynamism, more akin to learning or healing or growing. If you skid while riding your 12-speed, for example, and fracture your leg, your orthopedic surgeon doesn't write a prescription for a new tibia and send you home cured. Rather, he sets the break, puts on a plaster cast, gives you a pair of crutches, pats you on the shoulder, and says, "If we're lucky, it might take ten to twelve weeks." Like healing, *discerning directions is a process, not a product*. It takes time.

If you have picked up this book hoping for an instant answer to the riddle of your life or a "trip ticket" to your new career, stop reading right now. This book is not for you. I can't chase away all of life's uncertainties and ambiguities. But I'll try to add to your understanding of discernment, and if you would like to begin learning how *to identify the human and sacred signs* that hint at your new directions, if you are comfortable with a *process*, rather than a highlighted AAA road map, read on.

THE ROAD TO DAMASCUS

I suspect one reason we find it so difficult to think of career discernment as developmental, rather than dramatic insight, is because of St. Paul and what happened on his famous trip down the road to Damascus. He was knocked flat, saw a light, heard a voice, and there it was—a new life, a new beginning, a clear new direction. Or so it seems.

But was it all that easy? If you think about it, even in Paul's case what happened seems more like a fog lifting, a haze slowly burning off in the morning sunlight, a gradual healing, rather than a sudden change and a clear vision of the future. For example, after Paul got up from the ground, he was blind. All he knew for certain about his future was that he should continue on in the same direction. So someone took him by the hand, and Paul stumbled on down the road toward Damascus. Somehow he found a place to stay in a stranger's house. There he met Ananias, who at first didn't quite trust him. But through Ananias's help, Paul recovered his sight and was received into the early church.

Paul's life started to change, slowly; he was full of enthusiasm, but even then his direction wasn't very clear. So Paul did what seemed to make sense—he stayed in Damascus and started preaching, began telling people his story of what had happened on the road. Soon his actions stirred up such hostility within the non-Christian community that he was at risk for his life. So tense was the situation, in fact, that he was forced to escape from Damascus hidden in a basket.

Next Paul went to Jerusalem where he thought he would be among friends, but found, instead, that the Christian community was suspicious of his motives, even refusing to believe that he was a disciple of the Lord. Then Barnabas became his mentor and introduced Paul to the apostles. But Paul had no sooner settled into his new role, preaching to the Greek-speaking Jewish community, when he received more death threats and had to flee again.

And so it went. No easy answers about directions. No marked road map for Paul. Only confusion, false starts, mistrust, misunderstandings, and failures. A process and not a pre-packaged product.

A JOURNEY OF DISCOVERY

I like to think that by reading this far, you've already started on a journey of discovery, on your own road to Damascus. And do you know how I see myself? As that nameless person who took Paul by the hand, after he was struck blind, and guided him step by step down the road to a new life. He didn't push, this unknown mentor, didn't impose his own values; he didn't turn Paul around and send him back, say, to Jerusalem. Rather, he was a guide, a helper, a friend. I hope that's what I will be for you as, together, we explore your future directions.

A word of explanation: As you read further, you will notice that *Discovering Life's Directions* draws on two different sources—career consulting, and care of the soul (spiritual direction). I often use the term *discernment* which is properly a charism of spiritual guidance. And career management provides counsel concerning one's professional or vocational directions. Theoretically we can identify the individual functions, but I believe that we separate them in real life to the detriment of both.

Over the past year I have read most of the popular spiritual books on the topic of discernment. Most of these offer genuine insights on the subject for their readers. But, with a few notable exceptions, the spiritual books I read on discernment all shared the same limitation—an obvious lack of interest by the authors in what psychologists and career specialists have been saying over the past decades about the human factors involved in discerning directions. Any serious effort, it seems to me, to guide people spiritually in determining their paths also demands a thoughtful analysis and careful integration of all the human factors of the discernment equation.

I have known several career changers, for example, who prayed piously for the guidance of the Holy Spirit, but who didn't have a clue about even the elemental techniques of networking—by all standards the most productive source of new career information and employment interviews. I have heard of parish councils that, before their discussions, bowed their heads and asked the Lord for the grace of discernment concerning the parish's future directions, but who never bothered to learn the elementals of group dynamics. On the other hand, I have worked with many hard-charging corporate executives, pursuing an upward path within their company's hierarchy, who had become "empty suits," losing themselves in the process, because they never listened to the real hungers of their hearts, or discovered their own souls.

In the chapters that follow I will share with you the insights I have gained about reading signs, the process of discerning directions, from both a professional and spiritual perspective. From time to time, I will share my own tale—reluctantly—because some incidents in my life may illuminate and help you understand the events in your own.

WHO SHOULD USE THIS BOOK?

Discovering Life's Directions is addressed to any person considering a change in his or her career or facing a life decision. I am writing not only for church professionals, but for men and women of faith who would like their spirituality, their religious values, to affect their life-choices. I am thinking of the young lawyer, for example, who is weighing the conflict between the demands of partnership and parenthood, or the marketing executive balancing the time needed to cultivate a relationship and the extensive travel requirements of his or her career.

I am also writing, of course, for the woman religious who, after thirty years of teaching, now desires to discern a new ministerial direction—working in a shelter for battered women, say, or in an outreach program for recovering Catholics—those formerly practicing Catholics who are angry, searching, or returning. Or for the parish priest, approaching sixty, who is hearing the faint, far-off strains of "September Song" and is wondering how he can most productively and creatively proceed with the next phase of his life. So this book is for deciding major life directions as well as minor lifestyle choices, such as whether one should live in a traditional convent or rectory setting or in an apartment with a small community of like-minded colleagues. *Discovering Life's Directions* is for anyone, lay or religious, in any period of "transition," who needs assistance in making a spiritually insightful decision about future directions.

HOW TO USE THIS BOOK

Discovering Life's Directions is designed to be used in several ways:

- *As an individual guide.* You can read the whole book through, from cover to cover, and then go back and do each chapter separately. Or you can start from the beginning and complete the exercises in each chapter. I recommend the second method as the better choice. Set aside some time each day for a couple of weeks, perhaps twenty minutes each day at lunch time or in the morning before you go to work.
- *As a source book for a weekend retreat and as a personal career planner.* In fairness to yourself, however, don't speed through the text. Take time to reflect on what you read. And above all else, don't skip the exercises. *Discovering Life's Directions* is designed to be *experienced* as much as read, and the exercises are an integral part of your personal journey of self-discovery. They will provide you with much food for thought.
- *As a resource for a spiritual support group.* The material in *Discovering Life's Directions* is also designed to be used for adult religious education. I suggest that you find two to a dozen other people who are interested in meeting for about two hours a week for a six-to-eight-week period. Begin by reading aloud the focus part of each chapter, and then have each one in the class do the suggested exercise individually. Next, break up into small groups of two or three and ask each participant to share with the other members of the group his or her completed exercise. Talk over each participant's contributions and insights and, finally, spend a few minutes praying together using the suggested format at the end of each chapter.

THE CHAPTER OUTLINE

You will notice that each of the chapters that follow is divided into five parts: an introductory *Reading*, then sections titled *Focusing, Reflecting, Discerning,* and *Praying.*

Reading

I introduce each chapter with a passage from some piece of literature, usually about a person at a particular crossroads of his or her life. The intent is to set the theme and define the direction of the material that follows, but the reading also serves as a way to focus our attention and center our imaginations. Read this section slowly, carefully, thoughtfully. Use the reading to create a quiet, meditative moment and turn your attention inward as you begin each chapter.

Reading great literature, Frederick Buechner suggests, in his book *Listening to Your Life*, is like looking into someone else's picture album. There is always the possibility that among all those photos of people you never knew or places you never visited, you may come across something or someone you recognize. As the pages flip by, you catch a glimpse of yourself. The story of any one of us is, in some way, the story of us all. I hope you will read each introductory reading carefully, even aloud, and in the reading, hear your own voice.

Focusing

Focusing is the informational part of each chapter. It introduces the chapter topic, presents some ideas, and offers insight about a particular aspect of your career search and spiritual journey. It is not intended to be the last word on the topic, only an opening for a conversation, for discussion among friends.

I should say a word here about Sara Hughes, the major character in this book. Sara, you will soon discover, is the liturgy coordinator for a suburban parish in the Midwest. She is a fictional character, a literary device, but the circumstances of her life and ministry reflect the journeys and career concerns of many different people from all walks of life. In some sense Sara has become alive, so real, in fact, that a lawyer friend, who read an early draft of this book, called me and proudly announced, "I think I know the real Sara Hughes. She's the director of adult education in the next parish!"

I introduced Sara in an early chapter merely as an illustration, but as I continued writing Sara elbowed her way into subsequent scenes and situations. Her character soon took on a life of its own; now she's in the whole book. Sara provides continuity from chapter to chapter and, by her struggles to define her directions, illustrates perfectly the weaving together of a contemporary spiritual journey and career change. Thank you, Sara, wherever you are.

Reflecting

The reflecting part of each chapter contains a simple exercise that is designed to assist you in gaining a different perspective on your life's journey. It is important that you don't skim this section, but take as long as you need, not just to read, but to actually *do* each exercise. One of the intriguing aspects of a visual image, or a picture in portraying your life, is that you are thus enabled to find more than one insight or more than one meaning in the story of your personal journey.

Discerning

Discerning flows naturally from reflecting. This section is written to stimulate thought and insight. Think through your answers and then write them, perhaps in a notebook. If you are sharing your reflecting exercises with a small group, or even one other person, these discerning questions can serve as a catalyst to discussion.

(Note: A number of exercises and questions in the Reflecting *and* Discerning *sections require writing. Plan to have a notebook handy for that purpose.)*

Praying

This section may be a meditation from a gospel scene or a suggested personal prayer. Remember that Christians always have read the events of our Lord's public life, not only as a source of information about Jesus, but as an incentive to prayer. Recall the time when the Lord was moving through a crowd of people and a woman approached him seeking a cure for a chronic illness. She was too shy to ask him publicly for help, so she reached out and furtively touched the hem of his garment. Power went out from Christ, and she was healed (Mk 5:25-34). Put yourself in the gospel scene, talk to the Lord as if you were reliving an event from the life of Christ, or, if a prayer, recite the words slowly, reflectively, with feeling. Either way, touch the hem of his garment and speak to him from the heart about your life's needs and your future directions.

THE JOURNEY WITHIN

I once read a deeply moving story by Galen Rowell, the internationally renowned nature photographer. Rowell and his wife had received an assignment from *National Geographic* to photograph the mountain landscape of Patagonia at the tip of South America. The couple packed their photographic gear; updated their immunization shots; obtained passports, airline tickets, hotel reservations, maps, and film. They also organized their home for their absence—canceled newspapers, arranged business projects, caught up with their personal correspondence, and generally put their lives in order.

Two days before their departure date their editor called, said he was sorry, would still pay their fee, but was canceling the assignment to Patagonia. Rowell describes how they felt at first—disappointed and displaced. But then a strange thing happened—they suddenly felt energized and, freed from their ordinary routines, began to see their hometown from a completely different perspective, in ways they had never noticed. "I have a vivid memory," writes Rowell, "of running down a Berkeley street I'd been on thousands of times as the architecture of homes that I'd previously taken for granted jumped into my perception, as if some external voice were telling me what to look for."

More than this, Rowell and his wife noticed that they both seemed more open to new ideas and experiences; they had a view on their lives similar to the perspective usually received only after traveling a great distance away from home. For them the lesson was obvious: the renewal people receive from exotic travel is not so much from the travel itself as it is from the pre-travel discipline of putting one's life in order. Their insights were from within.

We are always making resolutions about renewing our lives and finding our true directions, aren't we? If only we had more leisure, we say, were with a special friend or mentor, could visit some sacred space—a Trappist monastery, the west of Ireland—or even had just a few days off to catch up on sleep and better organize our lives, then we would have the answers. Our way would be clear, our journey less cloudy.

Most of our lives don't provide such occasions. There isn't the time, or we waste the opportunities. But maybe it really isn't important for us to travel that far from home. May a careful, reflective reading of *Discovering Life's Directions* offer you the perspective you need—a chance to break the routine, put your life in order, gain a fresh view of your past and present, and discern that your pathway to the future is within.

ONE

Remembering: The Spiritual Journey

> My story is important not because it is mine, God knows, but because if I tell it anything like right, the chances are you will recognize that in many ways it is also yours. Maybe nothing is more important than that we keep track, you and I, of these stories of who we were and where we have come from and the people we have met along the way because it is precisely through these stories in all their particularity that God makes Himself known to each of us most powerfully and personally. If this is true, it means that to lose track of our stories is to be profoundly impoverished not only humanly but also spiritually.
>
> —Frederick Buechner, *Telling Secrets*

FOCUSING

Sara Hughes is the liturgy coordinator for a large, suburban parish in the Midwest and has gained considerable local recognition as an outstanding liturgist and church musician. Her pastor, Father Tom Cassidy, praises her work and credits Sara's efforts for the improved quality of worship at St. John's and the dramatic increase in weekend Mass attendance.

Sara has been liturgical minister at St. John's for almost five years. Fresh from Notre Dame with a graduate degree in liturgy, she was excited by the possibilities and challenges of her new job. But she was careful to introduce change slowly. Her first priority was building up trust among the St. John's community and becoming familiar with the style of the priest and people of her parish.

Next she inaugurated a training program for cantors, reassigned the folk group to a teen Mass in the school gym, hired a talented organist, introduced a richer musical repertoire, and reorganized the parish liturgy committee. New faces began appearing among the congregation and the choir. Parishioners would stop to compliment her after Mass and Father Cassidy, never overly generous with praise, began to credit Sara with creating a "worshipping community" at St. John's. He was also impressed by the increased Sunday offerings.

Soon Sara's efforts began to attract attention outside St. John's. She was asked to run worship workshops in neighboring parishes, speak at regional conferences, and was appointed to the Life and Liturgy Committee of the diocese. Recently she was approached by St. Catherine's, a local Catholic women's college, about teaching a course in a summer program of liturgical studies.

At a Crossroads

By every standard Sara is a highly-successful liturgist and dedicated lay minister. Yet recently she feels depleted of energy, finds herself too easily annoyed by the seemingly trivial concerns of the parish council and what she describes as Father Cassidy's lack of leadership. She also notices that it is harder and harder to get to work on time each morning at the parish center. As she explains it to a friend, "The people are the same, their questions are the same, and the answers are the same!"

So, at the peak of her career, Sara is at a crossroads and wonders about directions. While she has a great love of the liturgy and likes parish ministry, she no longer feels challenged by her job and experiences a vague sense of restlessness. Sara can't pinpoint any cause for her malaise. But she feels smothered at St. John's and realizes that there's nothing left in her position that she looks forward to doing. Everything has become routine. She's not even sure whether a move to another parish is the answer. After I set up the liturgy committee and introduce new music, Sara tells herself, it will be the same thing all over again. Is it time to move on? How does she decide?

No Easy Answers

Sara has shared her concerns with friends and received conflicting advice. Don Edwards, the director of religious education at her parish and a former seminarian, quickly diagnoses Sara's condition as a temporary occupational malady. He characterizes her uneasiness as the "itchy-feet" syndrome. "The people of this parish really need you," he tells Sara, and he advises that she "hang in there." Don assures Sara that most professionals have their down times and gray days, and if she perseveres in the performance of her duties, her ministry will soon become enjoyable again. Don recommends a weekend at a nearby retreat house.

Another friend, Camille Esperanza, a social worker, advises Sara that she has "paid her dues" to the church and that her own fulfillment is the most important factor in the equation. If Sara no longer feels challenged, if her career is stalled, insists Camille, then it's a clear indication that Sara should resign her position and move on to something more satisfying.

But Sara wonders if her ties to the Catholic community aren't something more than just "dues." What about commitment? Besides, as a forty-five-year-old single parent, Sara will probably have to start at the bottom rung of a new career and begin acquiring new credentials. Which way should she turn?

We will return to Sara Hughes throughout this book, but her dilemma about directions is echoed in the lives of many other people today. Consider, for example, the not uncommon situation of a professional woman in her forties who daily faces a work environment of almost continuous sexual harassment—suggestive language, casual touches, and a supervisor who openly promises promotions if she consents to sex. The woman could file a formal complaint, but she realizes that this action not only may bring embarrassing publicity but also cost her job. Should she blow the whistle and risk the consequences, or accept the situation, keep quiet, and protect her retirement benefits and needed income?

Men and women from all walks of life face choices about directions that seem to admit of no simple, clearly correct answers. Sometimes the crisis looms large and its solution involves a radical refocusing. On other occasions options are dramatically limited by past choices or present responsibilities, and the opportunities for change are relatively few. Again, some new paths become clear very slowly. Other career changes, however, are thrust upon us quite suddenly and when least expected. Many a business manager or sales executive, for example, has walked into work in the morning full of hope about the future, only to be "terminated" an hour later because of an impending merger or the unmerited animosity or ambition of a fellow employee.

Deciding Directions

How *does* a person of faith decide directions? What criteria should he or she use? The question is important, not only for those in a specifically religious career, such as Sara Hughes, but for men and women from all walks of life, from all business and professional backgrounds. How do people who desire to live ethical lives and make responsible choices weigh the multiplicity of factors in a major career choice and come up with the right answer?

Discerning directions is not "doing God's will" in the sense of popular piety, as if the whole of human history, past, present, and future, were like a carefully scripted and infinitely intricate play. In this scenario God is the playwright, producer, and director. Our task is to find a copy of the script, learn our lines, and play our part on the stage of life under God's detailed direction. According to this model of "doing God's will," discernment becomes a means of discovering that role, speaking our lines correctly, and giving the performance of our life.[1]

I believe, rather, that true discernment is more subtle, something like improvisational theater, where the actor, encouraged by the whispered comments and suggestions of the director, walks across the stage and interprets the role as it develops. The director, although recognizing that there are an infinite number of ways the part could be played, encourages and supports the actor in the unique interpretation he or she brings to the role.

Biblical Discernment

Scripture offers many insights and examples of the ways that men and women of faith turned to the Lord for guidance as they journeyed through life. In Old Testament times, discerning directions appears to have been a simple matter of asking and receiving a sign. For example, scripture describes how Gideon, seeking assurance of the Lord's loving care for Israel, put out a piece of wool, a fleece, on the floor of his tent and asked that in the morning the fleece would be moist with dew and the earth around it dry. The next morning Gideon wrung enough water out of the moist wool to fill a bowl, while the earth around remained dry (Jgs 6:37).

Again, Samuel, as a little boy, was brought into the house of the Lord and his future was determined by an answer to a direct request. It happened one evening when Samuel was awakened from sleep by a voice calling softly, "Samuel! Samuel!" Samuel, at first, did not understand who called and what was meant. He awakened Eli, the priest, to learn who spoke and how he should answer. "The Lord came and stood, calling as before, 'Samuel! Samuel!' And Samuel said, 'Speak, for your servant is listening'" (1 Sm 3:10). In time Samuel, too, was called by God to a sacred office and the vocation of prophet.

New Testament Examples

In the New Testament, in the days of his public ministry, Jesus would frequently cross people's paths, stride into their lives, and decide their new directions. "Follow me," he said to the apostles by the seashore, "and I will make you fish for people" (Mt 4:19). He called to Zacchaeus, who was sitting in a tree, "Hurry and come down; for I must stay at your house today" (Lk 19:5) And he carefully spelled out Peter's role in the apostolic community, "Listen! Satan has demanded to sift you like wheat, but I have prayed for you that your own faith may not fail; and you, when once you have turned back, strengthen your brothers" (Lk 22:31-32).

But with his resurrection, the Lord's presence became less direct, more discreet. To Mary Magdalene, visiting his tomb in the early morning twilight, he seemed at first to be a gardener; then Magdalene recognized him by the sound of his voice. Likewise, the apostles from their boat at first saw a man building a fire on a beach. They identified him as the risen Lord only after he had called to them across the water. Again, two faint-hearted disciples met a stranger walking along the road, and they were strangely moved as they listened to his words. Later, as the stranger sat with them at supper, the two disciples recognized him in the way he broke the bread. Then the Lord vanished from their sight.

So, if we are seeking a model of the way the Lord calls us today to new directions, it seems that he enters our lives in much the same way as he once called the prophet Elijah, who had fled for his life into the wilderness, escaping Jezebel. The prophet stood at the entrance of a cave overlooking a valley when the Lord passed by and a mighty wind tore at the mountain and shattered the rocks. But scripture tells us that "the Lord was not in the wind." After the wind, there was an earthquake and then a fire, but the Lord was in neither the tremor nor the flames. And then the Lord did speak, and Elijah heard him as a "still, small voice" (1 Kgs 19:1-12).

It is the same with us. The Lord comes into our lives as that "still, small voice." But as John Henry Newman observes, somehow we do not really believe it, we do not look for the Lord, or listen for his call as something that takes place today. We have neither the eyes to see the Lord, nor the ears to hear his voice. And we fail to hear less because of malice than because of so many other voices that clamor for our attention, so many other interests that compete for our consideration. As a result, we need a way of focusing, some method of attending to that "still, small voice" of the Lord, particularly concerning the choices we make over the directions of our life. Christian tradition calls that spiritual sifting of the true from the false, the authentic from the trivial, discernment.

I will use the term *discernment* throughout this book. But I do not mean the "discernment of spirits" of some spiritual systems, whereby a person examines alternating states of spiritual consolation and desolation; nor am I focusing on the biblical criteria for discerning true and false prophets. I am writing here, rather, of discernment simply as a judgment reasonable people make about their directions after examining their life experiences in conjunction with the insights offered by their religious traditions and faith communities.

How to Start

Where do we begin? If we are serious about change and are really seeking guidance to help us identify or define our new directions, it makes sense that we can't sit "all the day idle," waiting passively, either to be rescued by an angel, like St. Peter when he was in prison, or to be illumined by a blinding light on our personal road to Damascus. Rather, we must take the first step, no matter how tentative or hesitant, and begin making connections, at least through reading and research, with the appropriate resources that will help flesh out our dreams, define our goals, and start the journey toward our new directions.

We have to start somewhere. I have found that for many people even a *symbolic* action is a start. Something as simple as a visit to the local library, for example, to browse their resources and look up in their data bank some recent articles about a particular area of interest. We undertake this preliminary exploration, not only because the creative process begins with dreaming dreams about our future, but because we must begin sketching in the rough outlines of our new directions—not the complete picture, just a preliminary draft. One step at a time, to be sure, but that first step must be ours. It may not sound dramatic, and it is certainly hard work, but for serious career changers basic research is the beginning of wisdom.

God is never outdone in generosity. If we make even the smallest gesture in the Lord's direction, in his own time, and in his own way, he will show us the next step on our path. For most people that pathway begins not only with dreams about the future, but by also reviewing the past, examining their crossroads, the interests that excited them, the connections between that past and their present, the ways their life stories have unfolded.

The First Step—Listening to Our Life's Story

Discerning directions, as I view it, is really a two-step process—an interaction of our personal experience with the spiritual wisdom of our faith community. For the mathematically inclined, the chart on the next page shows how I would draw an equation of the discernment process.

First of all, the discernment equation includes a prayerful attention to our life experiences, a listening to the labyrinthine ways of the story of our life, from the first stirrings of our spiritual sensibilities as children, through our adolescent years, to the

The Discernment Equation

Life Experiences	+	Wisdom of the Christian Community	=	Directions
Our Stories:		*Newman's Windows*		
Childhood		Friendship		
Adolescence		Loss of a Loved One		
Adulthood		Scripture		
		Contemporary Literature		
		Defining Moments		

present moment in our adult journey. Our past is often the best predictor of our future, or in Marshall McLuhan's inspired phrase, we drive into the future looking through our rear-view mirror.

So subtle is God's saving power in post-resurrection times, in fact, that Newman lays it down as a general rule of discernment that the Lord's presence is most often noticed, not at the moment of his visitation, but only later. We notice him when we look back at this or that significant moment and recognize his hand in the circumstances of our lives. "Have I been with you all this time, Philip, and you still do not know me?" Jesus asks (Jn 14:8), and, again, he reminds Peter, "You do not know now what I am doing, but later you will understand" (Jn 13:7). Listen to your life's story, suggests Newman:

> Let a person who trusts he is on the whole serving God acceptably, look back upon his past life, and he will find how critical were moments and acts, which at the time seemed the most indifferent: as for instance the school he was sent to as a child, the occasion of his falling in with those persons who have most benefited him, the accidents which determined his calling or his prospects, whatever they were. God's hand is ever over his own, and he leads them forward by ways they know not of.[2]

The Second Step—Spiritual Windows

But memory and intuition alone will not provide an adequate basis for our spiritual decision-making. We need to inquire whether our desire for a new direction is compatible with our love for God. We must validate our personal experience in light of the spiritual wisdom offered us by our religious and cultural traditions. Among the many resources in our lives that hint of God's loving presence and suggest pathways and possibilities—the advice of a friend, for example, a chapter read in a book, the guidance gained through therapy—are the insights of the Christian community's greatest spiritual teachers. Among these are Ignatius of Loyola, Teresa of Avila, Francis de Sales, and John Henry Newman.

Although he was a nineteenth-century Englishman, Newman's busy life—the demands of his friends, the difficulty of his decisions, the complexity of his problems—reveals him to be a modern man deeply aware of the pressures of urban life and the multiplicity of intrusions and interruptions experienced as one moves, morning to evening, from conversation to conversation. A few of these moments are important; most are insignificant. In his spiritual teaching Newman suggests that among these random roads in life, and the many dead ends, there are some unique situations, which he calls "accidents and events," that are specific occasions for the Lord's call, windows through which his love enlightens our lives. Newman enumerated five kinds of special life events:

- Friendship
- The loss of a loved one through death or departure
- Sacred Scripture
- Contemporary literature
- Defining moments

Later in this book we will examine Newman's spiritual teaching about these special life events in great detail and see the reason he believed these five "windows" are particular moments in life where the Lord seems to overtake us on our journey and reveal his presence within our hearts.

Beginning the Journey

In the chapters that follow I am going to help you prayerfully examine your directions. We will begin by considering first the two major roadblocks that hinder many people today from making enlightened career choices: work addiction and passivity. Chapter Two investigates burnout and describes how it is, when work becomes all consuming, that the energy to sustain a ministry or even a career suddenly disappears. Spiritual burnout can happen to anyone, particularly those people with the greatest dedication and the loftiest ideals. It can happen as much in the local rectory or parish house as in the corporate executive suite. However much the conditions leading to burnout are encouraged by the prevailing business or ministerial culture, its symptoms warn us that we need to pull back for a time and perhaps even seek a new ministry or direction.

Passivity, the focus of Chapter Three, is at the opposite end of the spectrum. Not only can passivity mean total career immobility and chronic procrastination ("Why can't I get moving?"), but it sometimes also involves secondary avoidance activities, such as micromanaging or the compulsive writing and rewriting of letters and memos and course outlines; spending inordinate amounts of time playing with adult toys, such as short wave radios or computer networks; or tinkering with parish tasks that aren't priority concerns. As we will see, passivity often is accompanied by a rescue fantasy—"God knows what's best" or "The Lord will provide."

In Chapters Four, Five, and Six, we will reflect upon the significant events in our personal journey of faith—upon the stories from our childhood, adolescence, and adult years. We will examine these stories, not as mere memories but as narratives that reveal a relationship, not only with the events themselves, but with the transcendent Mystery they mirror.

Chapter Seven will examine the second part of the discernment equation, those significant moments that Newman, in his preaching and spiritual direction, identified as special windows of discernment. Those are the after-the-fact signs that the Lord is drawing us to him, those special hints he offers us about our future directions.

Chapter Eight ties together all the significant events of our spiritual life, from the dawning of consciousness up to the present and, by a simple time-line exercise, assists us in recognizing not only the mystery in each special moment, but the patterns and themes of the whole sweep of our spiritual journey.

Chapter Nine, "Testing New Directions," will provide some practical advice for validating our particular decisions about our directions. This chapter will also offer some suggestions for developing a network and soliciting the advice of friends in defining a particular career direction.

The Risen Lord

First, in reflecting upon the unfolding events and stories of our own lives, and, second, in listening to the spiritual wisdom offered us by our religious and cultural traditions, we really will be seeking the face of the risen Lord, who stands just beyond the veil of the present moment. Each reader, obviously, has journeyed to Christ along different paths; the events of our lives are dissimilar. But in some subtle ways I suspect that the patterns are strikingly the same. For all of us, there have been wanderings from childhood religious ideals and later returns, false starts and new beginnings, overwhelming failures and moments of ecstatic joy.

In Rostand's play *Cyrano de Bergerac*, Cyrano is infatuated with Roxanne but is so shy that he stands in the shadows under her balcony and speaks words of love that are mouthed by another suitor. Years later they meet; his love finally is revealed when Roxanne hears Cyrano speak "in such a voice that I remember long ago. So it was you!"

It is my hope that the readers of this book, as they reflect upon the patterns of their lives, may experience a similar moment of recognition—a sense that they have not been alone on their spiritual journeys. May they discern that at certain times along the way, like other faint-hearted disciples, a stranger overtook them and, although his identity was hidden from their eyes, spoke to them with that "still, small voice," in unexplained events and unexpected graces—a voice they now remember from long ago. "So it was you!"

REFLECTING

To assist you in evaluating your present career satisfaction, use this check list to compare your present attitudes towards your work with Sara Hughes's feelings about her position as liturgy coordinator at St. John's:

X = Sara's responses

✓ = Your attitudes

	Always	Usually	Now and Then	Rarely	Never
Low Energy at Work		X			
Frustrated		X			
Angry at Authority			X		
Everything Routine	X				
Drowning in Trivia	X				
No More Challenge		X			
Fatigued After Work	X				
Vegetating	X				
Seems No Way Out		X			

DISCERNING

1. After taking the above "snapshot" of your career situation, what do you see? How does your personal and professional satisfaction compare with Sara's?
2. Newman observed that the Lord's presence in our lives is often noticed after the fact, when we look back upon some significant moment or event and then recognize his presence. Has this ever been your experience? If so, what event or special moment in your past life do you now recognize as the loving care of God?
3. Marshall McLuhan observed that we "drive into the future looking through our rear-view mirror." What event in your past could serve as a predictor of a successful career transition in your future?
4. As a result of reflecting upon this chapter, what real or symbolic action will you undertake as your first step toward a new direction?

PRAYING

In 1833, returning from a trip to Italy, John Henry Newman had passed a critical crossroads in his life and reached a momentous decision about his future directions upon his return to England. Newman's boat had been becalmed for a week off the coast of Sardinia and one evening, as the wind finally came up, the foggy skies cleared, and the full moon was reflected on the waters, he composed the following poem. As you begin to examine your own career directions, read Newman's words slowly, prayerfully, and make his sentiments your own:

Lead, kindly light, amid the encircling gloom,
  Lead Thou me on!
The night is dark, and I am far from home—
  Lead Thou me on!
Keep Thou my feet; I do not ask to see
The distant scene; one step enough for me . . .

TWO

Career Paths and Work Addictions: Workaholism

For the past three years, I have worked 70 to 90 hours and seven days a week. I complained about it, but secretly I enjoyed it. I was an important person in a growing company. I was able to say something of myself that communicates in our society: I was busy . . . It felt good to be busy. People were impressed that I worked so hard—often until one or two in the morning. It is addicting. Like all addictions, it is also destructive. Over the past three years, my wife and I have noticed that we have little else in our lives or in our relationships. We have few friends. We had no contact with the city in which we lived. We were not involved in any kind of community. We would become furious if we were kept waiting by store clerks, delivery people, or friends.

"Where your treasure is, there will your heart be also." It became increasingly clear where our treasure was—in our jobs and in the heady pleasure of rapid career advancement. And our hearts began to shrivel—the inevitable result of selecting such a paltry treasure.

—Bill Peatman, *National Catholic Reporter* [1]

FOCUSING

I stayed in the city one evening to have dinner with a lawyer friend. By 7:45 p.m. I was on the commuter train, heading home and feeling vaguely guilty that I hadn't done any writing in the past few days. An investment banker type—a familiar figure along the route—slid into the seat next to me. Immediately his briefcase clicked open and I heard the tap . . . tap . . . tap . . . of his laptop.

Out of the corner of my eye I could see that he was writing memos for the office he just had left. I crunched deeper into my seat and read the sports page, wondering about the Phillies' prospects for next season.

Soon I heard electronic beeps. My seat mate was now on his cellular phone, closing a deal in Hong Kong, using financial language I don't completely understand like futures, arbitrage, letters of marque. This made me feel worse, because I neglected to refinance my mortgage when rates were low. The deal completed, he phoned his partner, his secretary, and finally his wife at her office. When the train pulled into our station the briefcase snapped shut and my companion strode down the lane to his home, while I shambled off into the night, still feeling guilty, wondering why I never invested in tax-free municipal bonds.

Work Addictions

The investment banker on the commuter train is a symbol of an apparently all-consuming corporate career. Burnout, such as that described in the introductory reading, is not uncommon among business professionals, even those in the helping professions. In fact, the term was first used to describe the state of emotional fatigue experienced by mental health professionals who tried too hard to "save" or rehabilitate their clients.[2]

Generally, burnout has three components—physical, emotional, and spiritual exhaustion. Physical fatigue is characterized by low energy and chronic tiredness. Emotional exhaustion involves feelings of helplessness, hopelessness, and being "trapped." Spiritual exhaustion is accompanied by a loss of meaning and a sense of futility over our vocational or professional path. Attitudes of "What's the point?" or "Why am I doing this?" sometimes also surface, coupled with negative feelings toward work, personal relationships, life in general, and even ourself.

I also have noticed that burnout often follows an obsession for work. Just as one becomes addicted to alcohol or drugs or gambling, so with the "workaholic" there is also a need for a "fix"—in this case, more work. My clients suffering burnout also show that "narrowing of focus" exemplified in the opening reading. These men and women have little time for anything else in their lives—

family, friends, committed relationships, or community involvement. Work is everything.

A vice president of a troubled computer company, for example, has written that her work became so all-absorbing, her sense of extreme urgency about her job so overwhelming, that her commitment to her career contributed to a troubled personal life. One year, between Labor Day and Thanksgiving, for example, this woman was able to take off only a day and a half from work. She missed her daughter's school plays, science fair, and teacher conferences. "I used to love cooking," she confessed, "but I stopped because I didn't know where anything was in my own kitchen. It was not my kitchen anymore. My house was not my house."[3]

Only Being and Breathing

In its extreme form burnout can result not only in a one-dimensional life, but in complete emotional exhaustion. An article in the *National Catholic Reporter*, by a religious woman in a very demanding social justice ministry, described how she was having tea one afternoon with a friend. Sister was simply too exhausted to continue and laid her head on the restaurant table, literally unable to move. The article went on to describe the antecedents of her burnout:

> When I first entered religious life about 30 years ago, I was told on the first morning to bring a pamphlet from the convent library to read during meditation time. I am a fast reader, so I went through mine several times. One phrase in it stayed with me: "There's plenty of time to rest in heaven; there's plenty of time to rest in heaven." I built my life around that phrase and the attitude it contained.
>
> Work hard I did; success in my work I achieved. And because I worked hard and was a success, people admired me, even loved me, or so I thought. And because I worked hard and succeeded, God loved me and admired me, so I thought. That was my formula for living and, I guess, for sanctity. That was Fran Dempsey, valued by me, valued by others, valued by God.
>
> Such efforts to work and achieve, efforts to give love so one can earn love, take energy. But what does one do when, in the prime of one's active life, the energy to sustain all that

achieving and loving disappears . . . ? What becomes of Fran when she stops dead, but not really dead, in her tracks? When all she's got left to show for herself are being and breathing?[4]

Burnout in Ministry

In my experience, parish ministers and religious professionals, as much as many a corporate executive are prime candidates for burnout, especially if their motivation for ministry is to earn the love or esteem of others or if they don't provide themselves emotional "safety nets" for sufficient nurturing. One example is the parish priest who is always on duty, serving as the rescuer for every stray and troubled soul he meets, even when on vacation. Another illustration is the woman religious, retired from teaching, who undertakes a new half-way house ministry for battered women and their children without establishing some minimal contractual understanding limiting her participation to a fixed length of time, say, an eight-hour day, four days a week. If she does not also provide herself with the opportunity, on a regular basis, for enriching and rewarding outside activities, such as art, dance, and personal friendships, should we wonder if later all she has left to show for herself "are being and breathing"?

There is a sense, too, in which certain ascetical traditions and spiritual folklore created a climate in the past that legitimized self-destructive behavior in the name of Christian ministry. I remember one such instance, long ago, on a retreat. During the question and answer period a woman religious asked the retreat master about the problem of "burning the candle at both ends" in her ministry. He avoided the real issue by the condescending reply, "Sister, dear, we should worry less about burning the candle at both ends, but rather be concerned with how brightly our candle shines!"

In fact, Diane Fassel has written in her book *Working Ourselves to Death* that there is a certain idolatry of work, not only for the compulsive corporate executive, but even for people in ministry, and nothing can come before this new golden calf:

> Pastors and rabbis are expected to sacrifice themselves and their families. Churches think nothing of asking them to work seventy, eighty, or even ninety hours a week, although the Alban Institute believes fifty-five hours per week is the

> maximum a pastor can work and still be effective. I remember a workshop for professional church workers in which I was airing some of my ideas about work addiction. I met the greatest resistance from the ministers. Exasperated, one of them blurted out, "It's not OK to kill myself for work, but it is OK to kill myself for Christ." I asked him to consider why God needed his workaholism, and to check out the idolatry of *his* god illusion.[5]

Addiction or Commitment?

But this raises further questions: Is the investment banker on the train—or the tightly-scheduled bishop in the local diocese—work addicted or self-actualized? How *do* we discern between the compulsive fast tracker for whom life is work and the committed person who simply loves what he or she is doing in a professional career or ministry? Work for the highly motivated and self-actualized individual is obviously very different from that of the workaholic. One is a path to personal and spiritual development; the other, a treadmill to burnout. How do we tell the difference between the two?

An excellent test is the scriptural advice about the good and bad fruit: "Every good tree bears good fruit, but the bad tree bears bad fruit," the gospel tells us. "A good tree cannot bear bad fruit, nor can a bad tree bear good fruit. . . . Thus you will know them by their fruits" (Mt 7:17-18, 20). Surface similarities certainly abound—the same long hours, the same intensity of effort, the same commitment to goals—but each work style presents a completely different set of motivations, values, and "fruits."

Work addiction, in addition to fragmenting the personality and narrowing the focus of outside interests, becomes all-consuming. It gives birth to a multiplicity of destructive and negative emotions and behaviors, such as a "hard driving" demeanor; anger; emotional isolation; rigidity; an explosive temper; an unwillingness to accept criticism; the urge to control; and a proprietary exploitation of employees' time, talents, and contributions. But obsessiveness is the primary characteristic because:

> For the work addict, the job is like a chocolate factory for an overeater. It is as if an active alcoholic were going to work in a saloon. Whether your workaholism takes the form of work,

rushing, busyness, or caring, the job is fertile soil. . . . What is more, you get paid for it. This is the addiction that is rewarded. There is an illusion that workaholics do not hurt anyone and they are good for the company. These ideas are not supported by the facts. Workaholics hurt themselves, others, and the company.[6]

The committed person seems to perceive work as a creative, graceful, present-moment experience. There are certainly times when the healthy worker puts in overtime or becomes absorbed in a particular project, but work is only one component and it enhances life; the workaholic is unable to say no to work and, as a result, his or her life is diminished. The highly motivated or self-actualized individual is able to integrate all the elements of life into a whole, "has light" in himself, to use Schweitzer's phrase, can laugh at herself, has a great tolerance for ambiguity, a willingness to listen, and possesses an attractive, wholesome, luminous personality that does not require approval, status, or the need to control others.[7] "You will know them by their fruits."

Sara's Situation

What Sara Hughes seems to be experiencing at this stage of her career is not so much work addiction or burnout, but actually the pain of growth. Someone who suddenly finds herself no longer professionally alive, or feels strangely inhibited in a certain career path, is like a person trying on a long-forgotten sweater or skirt from the back of a closet. There is a sudden discovery that one's frame has filled out over the years. All life is growth, not only physical but psychological and spiritual. This growth, however, can go unnoticed for a time and when discovered is often accompanied by its own stresses and its own pain.

It has long been recognized that creative people and high achievers, such as Sara, pass through certain predictable steps or stages in their professional life. I style this phenomenon the vocational "Rule of Thirds." Dr. Adele Scheele, a career management consultant, has characterized it as the "Learn-Do-Teach" career cycle. However you describe it, a career path often seems to follow three developmental phases, although these are not necessarily divided into equal time spans.

The "Rule of Thirds"

The first phase of one's time in a new position, *learning,* is spent in ascertaining how to carry out the basics of the job competently and professionally. Notice that Sara Hughes very wisely spent her early days at St. John's in getting to know the territory; establishing priorities; managing her time; and becoming acquainted with the parish community, its people and its pastor, through listening sessions and informal conversations. She had a pastoral plan, a general idea of how she would approach her new parish and the programs she would introduce. But Sara also listened and was open to suggestions. She was willing to learn.

After identifying the needs of her parish, Sara began to build upon what she had learned, fine-tuning the process and putting her own stamp on the parish programs and liturgies. This phase took a few years. Sara seems to have completed the middle third of her job cycle, characterized as the *doing* phase. She introduced new music, de-emphasized the old folk Mass, created a new liturgy committee, added professional musicians as cantors, trained lay readers, and insisted upon certain standards of performance and dress for the various parish ministries.

The third phase that a person spends in a particular position is the teaching phase, where the professional, having learned the basics and left his or her own mark on the position, now goes out to others as a mentor, an expert, a presenter, a consultant, or a facilitator. This can happen in any number of ways. He or she may begin to write, make presentations at seminars and professional meetings, or offer courses in a particular field. Notice how Sara's horizons have recently begun to expand beyond St. John's, first at the diocesan level, then in academia.

Like Sara Hughes, many people today experience the "learn-do-teach" cycle in their professional lives—whether they are corporate executives, marriage counselors, management consultants, or teachers. At the human level a church ministry, or a call to social service, follows the same patterns of growth as other career paths. The caring professions mirror a similar human process; they are not exempt from the risk of burnout and work addiction, or from the signs of growth suggested by the experience of the career "Rule of Thirds."

No Clear Boundaries

Of course, in real life these career stages may not be that clearly defined; often they overlap. For some professionals, growth occurs slowly. Moving through each phase can be difficult both spiritually and psychologically. At each point in the cycle, a person is assuming new roles, practicing unfamiliar skills, taking risks—all factors tending to trigger understandable anxieties and moments of self-doubt. "Learning the ropes" in a new position, for example, may prove traumatic either because the individual proceeded too quickly in introducing change, or because there was a failure, on the part of both the employer and the new employee, to clarify mutual expectations.

So there will be times when career development means two steps forward, one step back. People often spin their wheels in a particular phase of the cycle, forced by the circumstances of their job to run in place like a gerbil on an exercise wheel. Or perhaps their whole career cycle may be complete and they find that they are unable to succeed in an impossible situation, or unwilling to move forward, although they are productive people who thrive on challenge and opportunity. It is then that they begin to experience the symptoms of career burnout, as described by the personal narratives earlier in this chapter.

For high achievers, and most professionals, when the third phase of the career cycle is completed, when the circle is closed, or when that work becomes the only thing in life, it is time to move—move in the sense of either shifting their focus toward another aspect of the same job or considering a new career path.

I am not, of course, recommending change for its own sake, because some people enjoy their chosen paths, maintain their sense of perspective about work, and know that they belong in law, or digital electronics, or campus ministry, or whatever. A person should develop in an understanding and appreciation of his or her professional career or ministry. But when people begin to sense that nothing in their present position excites them, when routine sets in and they begin feeling pain, or conversely, when work becomes the only thing in their lives, then they should reexamine their priorities and explore other possibilities.

Mother Theresa's Career

The lives of holy men and women are frequently the stories of people whose sense of their vocations grew far beyond the career paths they originally chose. Consider, for example, the example of growth that occurred in the spiritual commitment and mission of Mother Teresa of Calcutta. Although born in Yugoslavia, Mother Teresa entered the Sisters of Loreto in Dublin in 1928. From Dublin she was soon sent to India as a teacher of relatively-affluent European children and some native Indian students at the Loreto Convent School in Darjeeling. After a short while she was assigned to teach history and geography in Calcutta at a spacious and respected English school, also run by the sisters of her community. She eventually became principal of this school.

But in 1946 Mother Teresa received what she believed was a distinct call to leave the Sisters of Loreto and work among the poor. Humanly speaking, her circle was complete. Two years later she received permission from Rome to live out this new dream. She exchanged the habit of the Sisters of Loreto for a simple white sari with a blue border and began a new life and a new mission among the poor and needy in the Calcutta slums. One religious career had ended; another had begun. Mother Teresa later described her departure from the Sisters of Loreto as a "call within a vocation." It certainly was a call, but it was also a new career.

REFLECTING

At a career development workshop Sara heard about the "Rule of Thirds" theory and learned a way to diagram her own professional growth at St. John's. She first drew a circle, estimated the proportion and length of her learning, doing, and teaching cycles, and then, using a simple code, filled in the significant events, both positive and negative, of her career at St. John's.

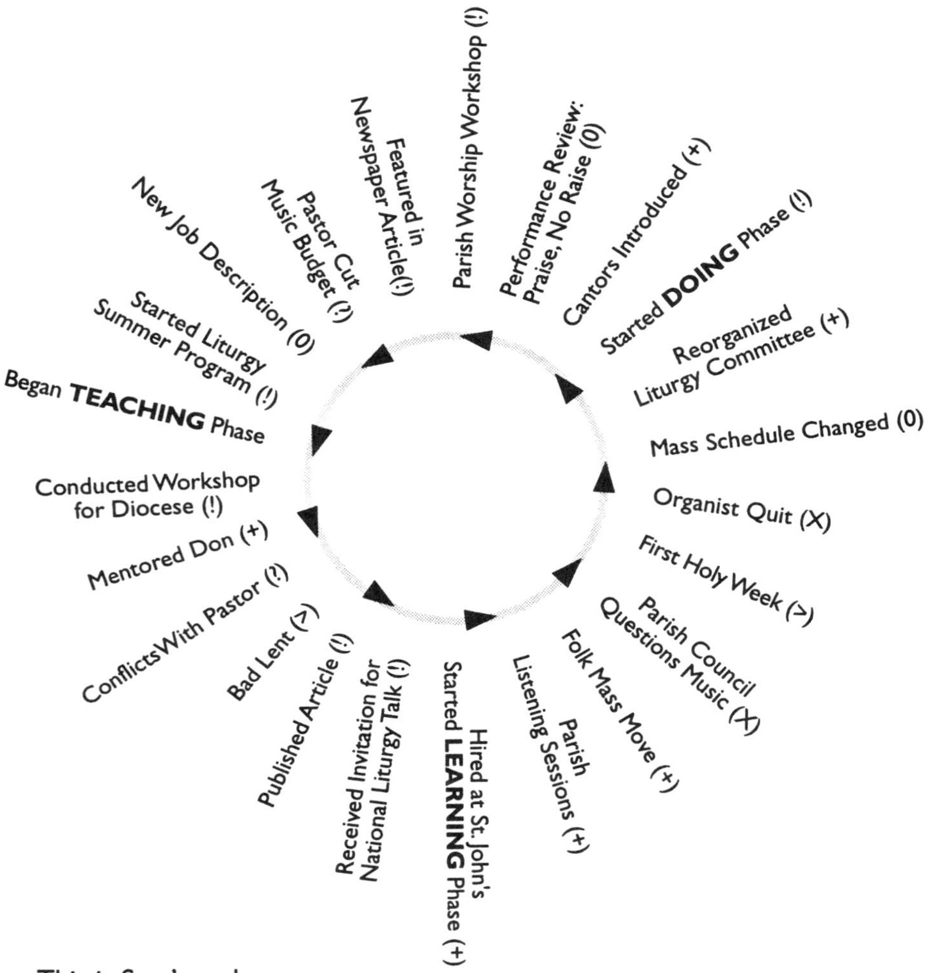

This is Sara's code:

- ! Times she felt the happiest and most satisfied with her career direction or job performance.
- X Points where she felt frustrated because of obstacles.
- ? Moments of her greatest self-doubt.
- O Times of annoyance over decisions made by others.
- + Projects that were gratifying.
- # Points where she felt bored or "spinning her wheels."
- > Times of physical, emotional, or spiritual exhaustion.

Draw a circle in your notebook using Sara Hughes's career cycle at St. John's as a model. Indicate the approximate phases (learning, doing, and teaching) of your present employment or career cycle. Estimate the date when you entered each phase. If your circle isn't yet complete, mark your career path up to the present time and indicate approximately when your circle will be complete. Using the symbols from Sara's code, indicate significant events and the quality of each of these events.

DISCERNING

Now go back over the exercise you have just completed and ask yourself these questions:

1. As you reviewed your career cycle, did you discover any patterns that surprised you?
2. What were your hopes and aspirations when you first took your current job?
3. If you could start over, what one thing would you do differently while transitioning through the learning, doing, and teaching phases?
4. What kinds of activities do you find most enjoyable? Most frustrating?
5. What are the three most stressful aspects of your work?
6. Identify the one most significant factor that has inhibited your smooth transition from one phase to another in your present position?

PRAYING

Make a tight fist of your hand, as you did when you were a child grasping some precious, beautiful thing. Then imagine your mother prying open your fingers and making you look at what you have been holding. Maybe it was a beautiful ladybug when you closed yourself around it; now it's lost its vibrance. So you let go, partly because of the forces that opened your clenched fist, partly because something once beautiful and yours is lost.

But now relax your hand; let it take its natural cup shape. It is a space, ready to be filled with something held more gently, that others can see, share.

As I look at my open hand now, I see that I hold a new knowledge of God, a new experience of God; I hold being me and allowing others to be themselves; I hold peace with my religious community's diminishment of its old kind of energy and its taking on new kinds of energy. I hold writing. I hold this moment. I hold this gift you give me of receiving my story. I hold this gift I give myself of relinquishing my story to you.

—Francine Dempsey, CSJ[8]

THREE

All the Day Idle: Passivity

When he woke up it was dawn. He woke with a huge feeling of hope which suddenly and completely left him at the first sight of the prison yard. It was the morning of his death. . . . He caught sight of his own shadow on the cell wall: it had a look of surprise and grotesque unimportance. What a fool he had been to think that he was strong enough to stay when others fled. What an impossible fellow I am, he thought, and how useless. I have done nothing for anybody. I might just as well have never lived. His parents were dead—soon he wouldn't even be a memory—perhaps after all he wasn't really Hell-worthy. Tears poured down his face: he was not at the moment afraid of damnation—even the fear of pain was in the background. He felt only an immense disappointment because he had to go to God empty-handed, with nothing done at all. It seemed to him at that moment that it would have been quite easy to have been a saint. It would only have needed a little self-restraint and a little courage. He felt like someone who has missed happiness by seconds at an appointed place.

—Graham Greene, *The Power and the Glory*

FOCUSING

After Sara Hughes confided her discontent at St. John's to Don Edwards, the parish religious education director, he reminded Sara of her role on the parish ministerial team and how much the St. John's worshipping community needed her skills. Edwards suggested that she was experiencing a normal period of career fatigue and advised that she wait before making any final decision. He assured her that with time her enthusiasm and interest would revive.

Different Meanings

Waiting during a time of uncertainty about life directions can mean several different things. First, it may imply a *period of discovery*, a necessary time for sorting out, in which a person steps back from one path and actively attempts to determine a new direction to follow. Newman, for example, withdrew from his active ministry at Oxford in 1843, went on retreat in the country village of Littlemore, and waited for two years in prayer and reflection while he discerned the new course of his life's journey. This kind of waiting is a contemplative crucible, a catalyst for new life and spiritual renewal.

In mystical theology, as in the case of St. John of the Cross or Simone Weil, *waiting* is understood as *a testing of faith*, a special grace accompanying a night of the soul, a "waiting on the Lord." This can be a frightening time of darkness in which the soul waits for God through a long, dark night. St. Thérèse of Lisieux described the terror of this kind of waiting, her fear that she had lost heaven, her "native country":

> Just as Christopher Columbus divined, by instinct, the existence of a New World which nobody had hitherto dreamt of, so I had this feeling that a better country was to be, one day, my abiding home. And now, all of a sudden, the mists around me have become denser than ever; they sink deep into my soul and warp it round so that I can't recover the dear image of my native country anymore—everything has disappeared.
>
> I get tired of the darkness all around me, and try to refresh my jaded spirits with the thoughts of that bright country where my hopes lie; and what happens? It is worse torment than ever; the darkness itself seems to borrow . . . the gift of speech. I hear its mocking accents: "It's all a dream, this talk of a heavenly country, bathed in light, scented with delicious perfumes, and of a God who made it all, who is to be your possession for all eternity! You really believe, do you, that the mist which hangs about you will clear away later on? All right, all right, go on longing for death! But death will make nonsense of your hopes; it will only mean a night darker than ever, the night of mere non-existence."[1]

Passivity

Finally, for others, *waiting* can have a more sinister meaning—it becomes *an evasion of responsibility*; it masks a habit of decision-avoidance that is detrimental both to a person's career and vocational well-being, and to his or her spiritual and emotional growth. This is the kind of passivity that Graham Greene's nameless "whiskey priest" accuses himself of on the morning of his execution—if only there had been "a little self-restraint and a little courage."

When we confront a problem about our careers or face decisions about future directions, we often feel at the mercy of unmanageable forces; we are afraid of running risks or feel anxious about the consequences. Procrastination is like driving with the emergency brake on. It is a low-level drag that can manifest itself in behaviors, attitudes, emotions, and relationships with others.[2]

Understandably, we are frightened by the possibility of change—moving to an unfamiliar residence, for example, working with new people, or accepting a position in a new state or across the continent—so we are tempted to sit tight, do nothing, and by default let someone else make our decisions for us. "Well, the personnel committee knows what it's doing," we say. Or, "The CEO is not going to let this company go bankrupt." Or, "The provincial has her reasons." Or, "The boss knows I'm doing a good job." This kind of waiting is synonymous with passive resignation. It is also often accompanied by a rescue fantasy.

The Rescue Fantasy

The rescue fantasy surfaces when people in difficult situations, particularly in dealing with choices about the direction of their lives, begin to indulge in dreams that some stroke of luck, like a lightning bolt from the blue, will suddenly intervene and resolve all their problems with a magical happy ending. Faced with insuperable financial burdens, for example, men and women conjure up scenarios about winning the lottery; overwhelmed by a dead-end job, they pin their hopes on a miraculous promotion or an unexpected offer of a new position.

Consider the case of a young lawyer—let's call him Dennis O'Brien—who has worked for five years in the go-for-the-jugular world of criminal litigation. Every day O'Brien strides into court to battle other lawyers, from one judge to the next, one jury to another. Always a new case to argue, new witnesses to impeach, new courtroom battles to win. Little by little he has begun to dislike his job. But never one to take charge of his life or actively seek other ways of doing law, O'Brien keeps telling himself, "This can't go on forever. Sooner or later things are bound to get better." The rescue fantasy neutralizes his ability to make rational choices. Until O'Brien takes control of his career, things will remain the same—or get worse.

Passivity in Ministry

Humanly speaking, the psychological dimension of a call to ministry is similar to the process of other career choices. Men and women religious enter their vocations as highly motivated people, full of hope for the future. They find meaning in their ministry as a transformation and consecration of all life to God by the leaven of holiness and their service to the members of the body of Christ. But after a few years a subtle change occurs. Some appear to lose their early ideals and settle into a holding pattern, preferring security to the risk—and the terror—of growth.

Passivity soon becomes habitual. These religious spend their energies maintaining the institutional status quo and preserving a style of life in which conformity and docility are primary values. When faced with choices, they decide that the safest path in life is to sit tight and wait. "God will provide" soon becomes a convenient rationalization for doing nothing.

God does provide, of course, but not as a divine magician or a Greek deity who descends from Mount Olympus with signs and wonders and rescues people from human responsibility. Rather, God comes to us as a friend, a lover, who calls us out of ourselves, who hints at directions but respects our freedom, who whispers ways and makes rough paths smooth. Even for those who feel trapped in impossible situations, whether a law firm or a religious community, there is always the surprise and unexpectedness of grace.

Some Examples

I once knew a middle-aged married deacon, a good and decent man, who was extremely overweight and always rumpled and slightly sad. One day our paths crossed in the supermarket. The deacon's color was better, he looked thinner, and his face almost glowed. "Frank," I said, "you look great. What have you done to yourself?" He proudly told me how the change had come about. Several months earlier he had been buying a new suit—a larger size—when he looked in the full-length mirror and, for the first time, saw himself as he appeared to others, a burnt-out, middle-aged man, portly and gray. "What have I become?" he asked himself, and the next day went to his doctor for a diet and began to exercise. His only regret: "Why did it take me so many years to see myself for the first time?" But as we parted, he smiled, "Better late than never!"

Another example: Grant, a priest ordained twenty-five years, was at the funeral of a seminary classmate. He had attended many priests' funerals before, but at the end of this particular liturgy, as the diocesan clergy filed past the open casket to give their last blessing, Grant noticed something very strange: His priest-friend had died suddenly while on vacation and looked extraordinarily peaceful, even healthy. But many of his surviving seminary classmates appeared dispirited and burnt-out. The corpse seemed in better shape than the congregation.

Grant knew of the sincerity and dedication in the lives of these good men. But he also recognized that many had long since ceased to grow, professionally and humanly. Their interests were limited, their lives circumscribed by the stifling concerns of their clerical culture. So they waited, as the years went by, for the next parish or a new bishop. Like them, Grant was also approaching fifty, but he still felt alive and was concerned lest he miss Christ and the meaning of his life "by seconds at an appointed place."

Counseling Sara

Sara Hughes did some serious thinking about Don Edwards' advice that she think twice and wait before deciding on a move away from St. John's. But is it necessarily virtuous, Sara wondered, to be passive in the face of career adversity?

Suppose my office was located in Sara's suburban town and she dropped by one day, told me her story, said she wasn't quite ready to leave her position at St. John's, but felt she should take a first step. I would not give her answers, but I would suggest that she consider certain possibilities and let her fill in the blanks. Here is what I might propose as a start:

1. Be good to yourself. If you are in one of the helping professions, perhaps take yourself as a client or a "ministry of one." Treat yourself as if you were the most needy client you know; be your own best friend. It sounds trivial, I know, but I saw that lesson lived long ago by a wonderful priest I once knew. It was his personal mantra. No matter what the topic of conversation, or the circumstances of our meeting, he would never say good-bye, but always part with those words, "Be good to yourself."

He practiced what he preached. Every Christmas my friend would buy himself an expensive present, have it wrapped, and put it under his tree. This behavior, I am sure, must have shocked some puritanical souls, but this good man understood the risk of emotional isolation for the celibate and explained his personal present this way, "If I don't take care of myself, who will?" So, the first idea I'd toss in Sara's direction might be this: Consider building time into each day for yourself alone and nurture your soul through music, exercise, reading, relaxing.

If you are inclined to be a rescuer, also learn how to say no gracefully. Learning such a simple social skill can be very liberating. Also, the more "down" people we work with professionally or ministerially, the greater the risk of catching the "negativity virus," and the greater our need for friends with a more realistic, positive view of life. Otherwise we will lose our sense of perspective, think of the whole world as negative, and forget that the goal of the Christian life is not Good Friday but Easter Sunday. My personal experience warns that we must be particularly wary of those one-sided, late night phone calls from friends, however needy, whose insoluble problems and incessant negativity become a drain on our time and energy.

2. Create some routines for defining your new directions. By routines I mean new behavioral patterns—something as simple as checking out the pastoral ministry want ads from the *National*

Catholic Reporter and testing your credentials against their criteria. Start a file of interesting career directions, including background articles on new ministerial interests, for example, experimental programs for "Recovering Catholics." Collect samples of resumes for future use, or browse the Wall Street Journal's *National Employment Weekly*, a rich source of advice and techniques on the process of career change. The exercises in this book also could be an excellent way to begin.

3. Do something, do anything. The antidote to inaction is action. Even some activity is better than none.[3] I am not talking here, as I was earlier, about obsessive tinkerers. I am thinking, rather, of chronically passive people. I have found that even an action as simple as sitting in a favorite work location, or even retyping a page of notes, somehow "primes the pump." We can promise ourselves that we will sit at our desk at home for just thirty minutes each evening, before going on to other things, and read some background material on our career "possibility list." This could be a book or even an article on parish ministry, desktop publishing, law school, franchising, or consulting—whatever topic or direction attracts our interest or inspires our dreams.

4. Don't be afraid to dream. Check the patterns of our negative, critical thinking; turn off the "Yes, but" tapes in our minds, and ask ourselves what we really want to do, where we really would like to be in the next five years. Examine the patterns of our life, past and present, as we will in the next chapters, and begin filling in the details of that dream and let it "pull" us into our future. Parker Palmer, the spiritual writer, describes the importance of dreaming dreams, in his book *The Active Life:*

> Every life is lived toward a horizon, a distant vision of what lies ahead. The quality of our action depends heavily on whether that horizon is dark with death or full of light and life. When we imagine ourselves moving toward the finality of death, our action may become deformed. We may become paralyzed, unable to act freely. We may become driven by fear, obsessed with protecting and preserving what we have, which is a sure way of losing it. With death on our horizon we may act in ways aimed at getting it over with, ways that lead to self-destruction now simply because destruction

seems inevitable. But when we envision a horizon that holds the hope of life, we are free to act without fear, free to act in truth and love and justice today because those very qualities seem to shape our destiny.

I suspect that these suggestions would make a lot of sense to Sara. She told me that among her favorite stories from the gospels is the tale of the landowner who leaves a certain amount of money to each of his three servants with the admonition, "Do business with these until I come back." One of the servants, fearful of the consequences of failure and hesitant about running risks, buries his inheritance and waits passively. The other two workers take the talents that the landowner has given them, make responsible choices, and turn a profit. As a result, upon their master's return, each earns his praise, "Well done, good and faithful servant" (Lk 19:17).

For Sara, the lesson of the gospel, as well as for life, has been clear, "Trade until I come."

REFLECTING

For a person wondering whether his or her career is stalled, it sometimes helps to identify some possible constraints or roadblocks inhibiting human and professional development. Test yourself with the following "Passivity Index." Each feeling statement flows from a constraint that hinders people from moving off center. While most constraints fall into three broad categories— emotional, behavioral, and cognitive—there is often overlap between the groups, so you may recognize yourself in more than one category.

This index lists feelings some people have when they are passive. Put a check mark (✓) in the column that describes how often you experience similar feelings.	NEVER	RARELY	SOMETIMES	MOSTLY	ALWAYS
1. I daydream about plans and possibilities but never take the first step.					
2. I am hesitant to explore new directions because of fear that I won't succeed.					
3. I get excited about new projects but then lose interest and give up.					
4. If I take a new direction or do something that sets me apart from my peers, I worry that I will be criticized.					
5. My life is disorganized.					
6. When I try something new, worry I will lose control of my life.					
7. I lack energy and feel tired.					
8. If my plans are not completely successful, I feel like a failure.					
9. Changing my career direction would upset my husband (wife, bishop, family, superior, friends, etc.).					
10. I am comfortable with things the way they are.					

DISCERNING

Review your index and circle the "high ticket" items; that is, those feelings you have reported as "Mostly" or "Always." Next do a "benefits analysis" of those high passivity feelings. Draw a line down the middle of a page in your notebook. For each of the high passivity items you have identified, list the advantages and disadvantages of that feeling. This list may indicate patterns and suggest to you why you are hesitating about taking more responsibility for your growth and your life.

PRAYING

Close your eyes and picture a warm summer's day. You are hot and tired and have been waiting for several hours at a country crossroads in the middle of a lush valley. Green fields stretch in all directions, and everywhere you look you see dozens of farm workers filling baskets, harvesting produce. A man in a long white robe walks down the road toward the place where you are waiting. It is the Lord. He looks in your direction, gestures toward all the workers, and asks with a smile, but still quizzically, "Why have you been standing here all the day idle?" "Because nobody hired me," you reply. You say the words, but they stick in your throat. Somehow they sound hollow. Talk to the Lord, as to your best friend, and in your conversation answer these questions,

Why *am* I idle?

What is my greatest obstacle?

Why am I waiting for others?

What is my first step?

What do I need to do?

FOUR

Falling Into Time: Childhood Experiences

In the living room the mail slot clicked open and envelopes clattered down. In the back room, where our maid, Margaret Butler, was ironing, the steam iron thumped the muffled ironing board and hissed. The walls squeaked, the pipes knocked, the screen door trembled, the furnace banged, and the radiators clanged. This was the fall the loud trucks went by. I sat mindless and eternal on the kitchen floor, stony of head and solemn, playing with my fingers. Time streamed in full flood beside me on the kitchen floor; time roared raging beside me down its swollen banks; and when I woke I was so startled I fell in.

—Annie Dillard, *An American Childhood*

FOCUSING

As a little girl, Sara Hughes grew up in the country and had often walked in the evening with her daddy. One very dark night he pointed up at the stars and told her a story about another little girl about the age of five, Thérèse Martin. Thérèse had gone walking out under the stars with her father and had noticed a faraway constellation that seemed shaped like a "T." Thérèse proudly announced that her name was written in heaven, and her father agreed.

After she had heard the story about that other little girl (now known as St. Thérèse of Lisieux) Sara would hold tight to her daddy's hand and search the constellations for a cluster shaped like an "S" to see if her name, too, was "written in heaven." Her father would look up at the night sky, and to his little girl's great delight, always point out a group of stars shaped "S" for "Sara."

Early Memories

Childhood experiences, such as walking under the sky on starry nights, gazing at saints in stained-glass windows along the side aisle of the church, the hissing of a steam iron, the feel of fresh sheets, and the thick smell of incense, may be distant memories, but they are never lost. For most of us, our first steps towards an adult faith have their origins in that shadow land of consciousness we call imagination, where symbols and stories, images and intuitions occur. How easy it must have been for Sara, having held tight to her father's hand on their walks under the stars, to imagine what God was like on another day when her mother first taught her to pray, "Our Father. . . ."

With good reason, then, scripture sings of the Lord's loving care from childhood, indeed, from the first days of our being,

> My frame was not hidden from you,
> when I was being made in secret,
> intricately woven in the depths of the earth.
>
> —Psalms 139:15

Scripture also affirms that God's loving care for us is even more tender than that of a mother teaching her child its first prayers,

> Can a woman forget her nursing child
> or show no compassion for the child of her womb?
> Even these may forget,
> Yet I will not forget you.
>
> —Isaiah 49:15

The Tenacity of Religious Images

The God revealed to Israel in the desert, the God of biblical faith, is unlike all the other deities worshipped by Israel's neighbors, the other nations and peoples inhabiting the fertile crescent at that time. The God of Israel is transcendent, as well as immanent in creation. God is personal, with a name and a love for each individual. This God meets us, as God met Israel, at the most precious moments of our lives, beginning with the time we were formed in the womb, nourished at the breast, and at all the significant events of our personal stories.

So important are the magic moments of childhood, in fact, that Andrew Greeley suggests that much of the religious sensibilities of adult Christians have their origins in the way the Christmas crib appeals to our imaginations as children. He observes that this is why the religious images of Catholicism are so deep and tenacious. A mother, for example, shows her child the crib that contains everything a little one of age two or three appreciates: a mommy, a daddy, a baby, animals, angels and men in funny costumes,

> Who is this baby? the little girl asks. That's Jesus. Who's Jesus? The mother hesitates, not sure of exactly how you explain the communication of idioms to a 3-year-old. Jesus is God. That doesn't bother the little girl at all. Everyone was a baby once. Why not God? Who's the lady holding Jesus? That's Mary. Oh! Who's Mary? The mother throws theological caution to the winds. She's God's mommy. Again the kid has no problem. Everyone has a mommy, why not God?[1]

If we don't pause from time to time to reflect on what was happening around us and inside of us as children, we run the tragic risk of losing touch not only with ourselves, but also with the God who was present to us in those precious moments. Discerning directions, then, begins by inviting the memories and stories of our childhood into our adult awareness, so that we may see how God's loving presence in our past has shaped and defined our present. By recapturing specific events and details from our past, we trace a thread from the known to the unknown. The path to our future starts with a trip down memory lane.

The Mohawk Martyrs

I must have been about seven when my mother, who was several months pregnant with my brother, David, spent a few days on a private retreat at the Shrine of the North American Martyrs at Auriesville in New York State. She had lost a baby two years before and was praying for a safe delivery. She took me with her on the retreat.

Auriesville is on a wooded hillside overlooking the Mohawk River; it is located on the site of the old Iroquois village of

Ossernenon. For a little boy, who had a vivid imagination and almost the whole rustic shrine and the reconstructed Native American longhouses to himself, this retreat was a magical week.

We met a young Jesuit while walking the shrine grounds, and he kindly offered to take me for a walk each afternoon while my mother napped. The young priest and I would hike down a trail through a nearby ravine, say a decade of the rosary, and then sit on a log in the middle of the woods where I would listen as he told hair-raising stories about the Jesuit missionaries, now canonized saints, who had once walked these same forest paths—Isaac Jogues, Jean de Lalande, and René Goupil.

The young priest described, while I sat there in wide-eyed wonder, how these brave Frenchmen had paddled down from Canada in their birch-bark canoes. They had been captured and tortured by the Iroquois, run the gauntlet, instructed the native children, baptized a few converts, and finally had been tomahawked and martyred. In fact, the priest explained, the body of René Goupil was never found; it probably lay buried somewhere nearby, a few feet from where I sat. I spent the rest of the week in the ravine poking the ground with a stick, looking for the bones of St. René Goupil.

The Wolf of Gubio

I have a friend, Maeve, whose spiritual journey began as a little girl attending a Baptist Sunday School and faithfully memorizing weekly Bible verses. Before she left for church each Sunday, however, Maeve would listen to a priest on the radio telling wonderful, imaginative stories to boys and girls about the lives of the saints: St. Francis and the wolf of Gubio, St. Thérèse and the roses, Father Damien and the lepers of Molikai.

Maeve's spiritual journey began and was nurtured by her Baptist church. Her pathways would take many turns, but in looking back upon her past, as an adult, she realizes now that it was those charming stories of the saints, as much as the memorized Bible verses, that captured the heart of a little Baptist girl. Maeve understands that in some way she was Catholic in her imagination many long years before she entered as an adult into full communion with the faith community of Francis and Damien and Thérèse.

The Interior Castle

Sue Monk Kidd has also described in *When the Heart Waits*, how childhood imagination and memory play a significant role in a person's adult spiritual journey. Kidd, doing a workshop exercise, was asked to draw a picture of a childhood experience. She sketched herself sitting in a sandbox building a castle. Suddenly, out of nowhere, a lost memory came floating back,

> I was around five. I'd built a sand castle in my sandbox and was searching for a flower or a pebble with which to crown the top of it. I walked to the mimosa tree and concocted one of those imaginary adventures for which children are famous: I imagined that there was a rainbow hanging upside down from a tree limb and that if I reached up and touched it, the castle in my sandbox would turn into a real castle. So I got on my tiptoes and pretended to touch the rainbow. . . .
>
> As the memory faded and I returned to the present, I was deeply affected—touched in an all-but-forgotten place. I sensed that those childhood moments of building a castle, touching an imaginary rainbow, and dancing around the tree held inside of them the most delight I had ever known or ever could know. It was that child who connected me to the radiant center of life.
>
> There in the workshop I thought about the book I had grown up to read: *The Interior Castle*, in which Teresa of Avila said that the soul is a castle through which we move to get to the Center. In an odd way, it seemed to me that the magical scenario I had concocted as a child was really true after all. When we touch the place where the rainbow hangs upside down—the inner child inside us—we find the real castle, the soul's castle.

A Doorway to Narnia

Even the most insignificant items from our past, such as a sandbox, can trigger memories and associations and have an enormous influence on our future. Author C. S. Lewis recalled how he and his brother had played as children in an upright clothing cabinet or wardrobe. Remembering that one piece of bedroom furniture triggered a flood of other memories and led to a series of children's stories about a wardrobe that became a doorway for other children into the magic land of Narnia.

These early intuitions of the sacred don't necessarily occur in an explicitly religious context. Notice how Annie Dillard depicts her moment of grace as happening one day when she sat playing on the kitchen floor of her family home. Suddenly she became conscious of life, which she describes as falling into the raging torrent of time.

Indeed, our earliest recollections are often linked to particular places and special settings. For Dillard it was the hissing of a steam iron, the banging of a radiator, and the rumbling of trucks on the street outside. For others it might be the feel of fresh sheets, the smell of baking bread, twinkling lights on a Christmas tree, or the memory of a sunlit room.

The Golden Stairway

Sunlit rooms always had their own special memories for Sara Hughes. One day, long ago, she was playing on the floor and, as dust danced in sunlight streaming into her room, she asked her mother, "Where's Daddy?" Her mother, with tears in her eyes, answered that Sara's father had unexpectedly climbed those golden stairs of sunlight to heaven. That moment would be relived many years later, as sunlight streamed into a different room, and a little boy would ask Sara, "Where's Daddy?" The setting would be the same, but this time the answer would be different.

Of course not all our childhood experiences are beautiful or positive. Some may have been very painful, and there may be memories, even of abuse, that hurt deeply, whose scars remain long after. The story of Thomas Merton's rejection by his mother—she would not see him in her last illness, but actually *wrote* her little boy a letter to say that she was dying—is such an example. But we encounter God in our sorrows as well as our joys and reflecting upon our past in the context of our whole life's journey, may cast even the painful events into a different perspective. The memories that hurt offer us an opportunity for healing.

But aside from painful memories, many of us are afraid, observes Richard Bode, that if we let ourselves remember the life that was, we will lose our composure. Our fear is misplaced, he suggests; what should frighten us more "is the possibility that we might lose the power to recall the life we lived, which gives us our connection to ourselves. Our most terrifying diseases aren't the ones that take our life; they're the ones that cast us adrift on an empty sea by depriving us of our memories."[2]

REFLECTING

You will need a pencil or some crayons and large sheet of paper for this exercise. Take as much time as you like and, using the illustration below as a guide, sketch a rough floor plan of your childhood home or your favorite room in that house. Don't worry if you make mistakes. Just be sure, as you recall your childhood house or room, that you include in your drawing everything that you can remember, including furniture, windows, pictures, favorite chairs, toys, appliances, bookshelves, desks, lamps, special mementos—anything that was a part of your early environment.

Now close your eyes for a moment and go back in time to the home in which you grew up. Imagine that you are entering the door. Walk through the kitchen. Notice the arrangement of the cupboards and appliances. Is anything baking in the oven?

Look at the kitchen or dining room table. How many places are set for dinner? Who sat around the table at Thanksgiving? Where is your place? Then walk into the living room or family room. Recall the position of the chairs. Where was the Christmas tree? Did you have a fireplace? What items were on the mantel? Did you have a front porch? Where was the downstairs closet? What was inside? Did flowers bloom outside your window?

Using a large sheet of paper, draw your own floor plan.

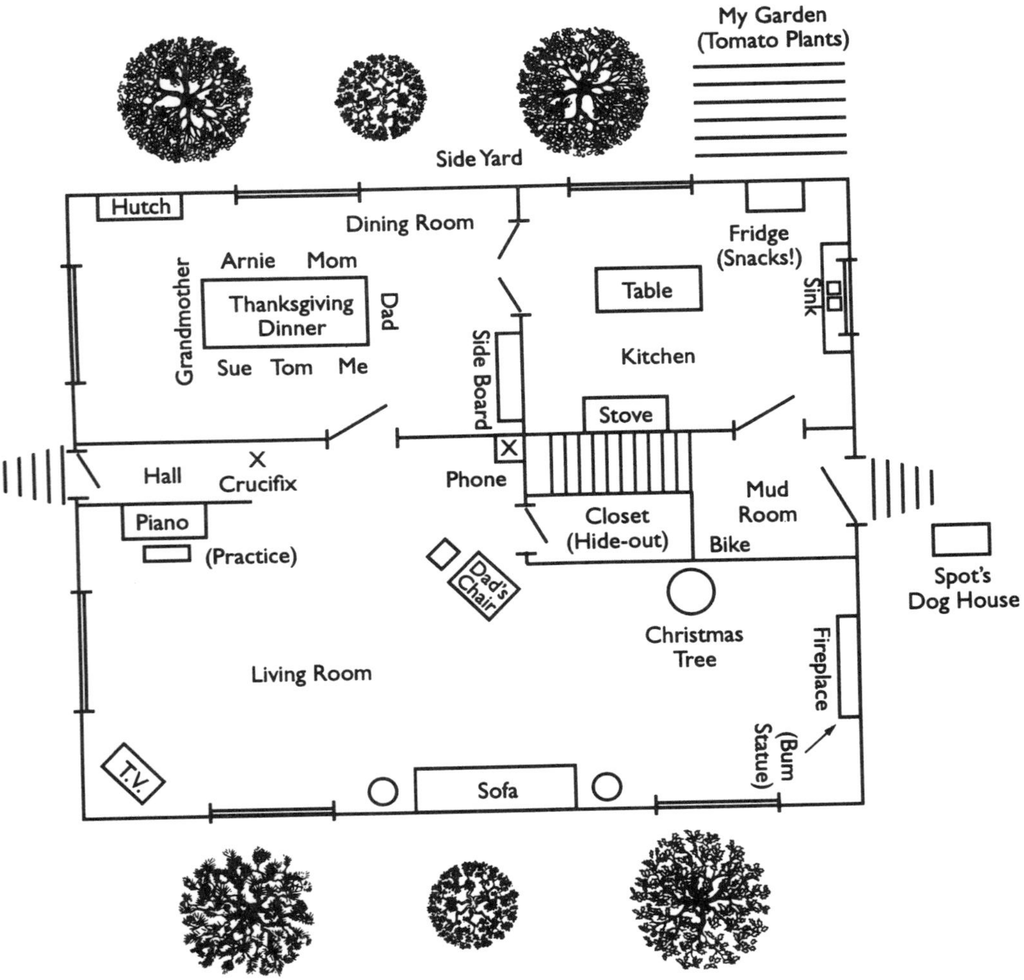
My Garden
(Tomato Plants)
Side Yard
Hutch
Dining Room
Arnie
Mom
Grandmother
Thanksgiving
Dinner
Dad
Sue
Tom
Me
Fridge
(Snacks!)
Table
Sink
Side Board
Kitchen
Stove
Hall
Crucifix
Phone
Mud
Room
Piano
Closet
(Hide-out)
Bike
(Practice)
Dad's
Chair
Spot's
Dog House
Christmas
Tree
Fireplace
Living Room
(Bum
Statue)
T.V.
Sofa

DISCERNING

Pretend that you are sharing your floor plan with a best friend or confidant. Visualize yourself welcoming your friend into that home or into your favorite room. As you walk through your house, describe each room in detail. Then answer your friend's questions about your childhood and the home in which you grew up:

1. What room was the center of family life? Which one is associated with your happiest memories?
2. Do you recall any special times in that house with your mother or father?
3. Did you have a hiding place or special area of play? Describe your favorite toy.
4. Which birthday do you remember the most? Why?
5. Did you have an imaginary friend? What was his or her name?
6. How was your home decorated for Christmas? Did your family have a creche? Where was it located?
7. What was the first prayer you ever learned? Did someone hear your prayers before bed?
8. What is your earliest memory about God or Jesus?
9. Annie Dillard "fell into time" one day as she played in her family kitchen. Was there a similar moment when you became aware of the sacred dimension of life—of God or Jesus? Where were you when it happened?

PRAYING

Begin by writing a two-page letter to someone you love—a spouse, a parent, a best friend. Tell the person a story about a moment of special awareness from your childhood. It doesn't have to have happened in church, or be explicitly religious like a first communion. Just describe a time when a sense of the sacred broke into your consciousness, when you felt loved or completely free, or when you realized that there was an Other in life—God.

Be present for a moment to that Other. Rest quietly in the Lord's love for a few minutes. Then, with all your heart, tell God of your love and your gratitude for the moments of special grace of your childhood,

> My frame was not hidden from you,
> when I was being made in secret,
> intricately woven in the depths of the earth.
>
> —Psalms 139:15

FIVE

Not Even a Sparrow: Adolescence

He dug the hole in a spot where there were no strawberry plants, before he studied the pigeons. He had never seen a bird this close before. The feathers were more wonderful than dog's hair, for each filament was shaped within the shape of the feather, and the feathers in turn were trimmed to fit a pattern that flowed without error across the bird's body. He lost himself in the geometrical tides as the feathers now broadened and stiffened to make an edge for flight, now softened and constricted to cup warmth around the mute flesh. And across the surface of the infinitely adjusted yet somehow effortless mechanics of the feathers played idle designs of color, no two alike, designs executed, it seemed, in a controlled rapture, with a joy that hung level in the air above and behind him. Yet these birds bred in the millions and were exterminated as pests. Into the fragrant open earth he dropped one broadly banded in slate shades of blue, and on top of it another, mottled all over in rhythms of lilac and gray. The neck was almost wholly white, but for a salmon glaze at its throat. As he fitted the last two, still pliant, on the top, and stood up, crusty coverings were lifted from him, and with a feminine, slipping sensation along his nerves that seemed to give the air hands, he was robed in this certainty: that the God who had lavished such craft upon these worthless birds would not destroy His whole Creation by refusing to let David live forever.

—John Updike, *Pigeon Feathers*

FOCUSING

In *Pigeon Feathers* the central character, David, a teenager of about fifteen, is suffering his first spiritual crisis. The boy had been reading H. G. Wells's *Outline of History*, when he is ambushed by the historian's dismissive description of Jesus as a political agitator, in a minor Roman colony, who somehow survived his own crucifixion and died a few weeks later.

With those words the fragile thread of David's adolescent faith seems to dissolve in his hands. And as Updike describes the process, David loses hope in heaven, pictures death as an extinction, and challenges the Lutheran minister at his Sunday School class about belief in the resurrection of the dead. Afterward, still in the torment of religious questioning, David desperately lifts his hands in the darkness of the night and begs Christ to touch him and heal his heart.

Later, David's grandmother asks him to use his rifle to rid the family barn of some nuisance pigeons. David complies, but as he is burying the dead birds, he notices the infinite variants of color and design in their feathers. And suddenly he experiences an epiphany, "that the God who had lavished such craft upon these worthless birds would not destroy his whole creation by refusing to let David live forever."

Updike's story intimates the fragile quality of adolescent faith and how a period of religious questioning is often a natural occurrence in the process, a road marker on the spiritual journey. Religious images, most often mediated to us by the values and example of our parents, are acquired early in life and their hold on our consciousness is tenacious. So the next step in the process of discernment is that we reflect not only upon our earliest religious memories—the stories and symbols that influenced our childhood—but that we also examine our adolescent years and discover whether the grace and beauty of these earlier images was affirmed or negated by subsequent influences and events.

Reconciling

The great spiritual and psychological task of adolescence is to reconcile the stern demands of life and the strictures of institutional religion with the grace and beauty of our earliest religious images. Beginning in adolescence, it is actually a life-long task and, for an impressionable teenager like David, the first occurrence of doubt or questioning can be agonizing.

Not all attempts to integrate earlier religious beliefs with our adolescent experience of life are as stressful and tension-filled as that experienced by David. Some spiritual moments of adolescence can be quite beautiful and actually affirm our childhood religious symbols and sensibilities. For example, during World War II my father was a combat surgeon with the Marines. My mother and father wrote to each other nearly every day throughout the war, but after the headlines disclosed a particularly bloody amphibious landing in the Pacific, my father's letters home ceased. Days later my mother received word through unofficial Navy channels that he had been a casualty. After hearing this news, she gathered our little family together around the dining room table and began an after-supper novena to St. Thérèse of Lisieux.

A "Sign"

St. Thérèse was a cloistered Carmelite nun of the last century (she died in 1897). She is called the Little Flower because somewhere in her spiritual journal Therese promised that she would spend her heaven doing good upon earth. She described that, metaphorically, by saying she would send a "shower of roses" to those who asked for her assistance.

In our novena, we didn't ask St. Thérèse for a miracle, only that we would know whether my father was with God or had survived the assault. The day after we finished our novena, the doorbell rang at supper time and there stood a neighbor—it was deep winter 1945—with a dozen long-stemmed red roses for our family. He hadn't heard my father was missing, and knew nothing of our prayers or St. Thérèse. He had just been driving by a florist shop that was having a sale and thought we would like the flowers.

Early the next morning our mailman called from the post office to say that he had just sorted dozens of backlogged letters from my father. He had survived the amphibious assault. My mother believed to the end of her days that the bouquet of roses did not happen by chance. It was, as she always described it, a sign. The childhood stories I had heard about mystery and miracles were also validated that dark winter's day with the bouquet of roses. Ever afterward, as an adult, God's loving care has seemed very real.

Integrating Parental Values

In the formation of a spiritual identity, an adolescent will typically sort out the social and ethical ideals handed on by parents, incorporate some aspects of their beliefs into his or her value system and, at least for a time, reject others. Writing in *The Call of Service*, here is how psychologist Robert Coles describes the process in his own life:

> As a child, when I heard my parents read to one another from *Middlemarch* or *Little Dorrit* or *Anna Karenina*, I also heard them discuss their "projects": my mother's Catholic Worker activism, my dad's far more conventional Community Chest activities. When I was a teenager, the last thing I wanted to do was read the novels my parents espoused so vigorously. I was equally uninterested in their "good works" . . . put off by, fed up with, a certain pietistic side of my mother, made all the more intolerable, I felt, by her insistence on putting her body as well as her voice on the line. I welcomed my father's more relaxed, even hedonistic view of life—and his sometimes profound doubtfulness, if not pessimism, about human beings and their prospects and purposes. Yet he too would yield to the pieties he heard from his wife and from Dickens, Hardy, and Eliot—and then take that next step toward community service himself.

Coles goes on to say that all he wanted in high school and college was to have a good time. But at some moments he felt the tug of his parent's values, their involvements. Later, he not only worked with Dorothy Day, the social activist, but lived for a time with her community among the homeless on New York's Lower East Side.

Sara's Adolescence

For Sara Hughes, moving from childhood religious ideals to the realities of adult belief was not nearly so dramatic. After the death of her husband, Sara's mother had gone back to work outside the home and much of the care of the little girl had come from her grandmother, whom Sara loved and admired. Nearly every Saturday, Sara and her grandmother cleaned the sacristy of their small parish church. Ever afterward, Sara would remember fondly the smell of stale incense and the color of the stained glass. It was here that Sara first learned to appreciate mystery and to believe in miracles.

Sara's first spiritual testing came when she entered an all-girls Catholic high school and became aware of the contrast between the simplicity of her early religious images and the demands of church authority as interpreted by the nuns of her school, St. Scholastica's. For example, the skirts of the school uniforms should not be hemmed too high, the sisters said, nor the necklines of the prom gowns cut too low.

In fact, spiritual formation at the school seemed fixated on sin and, in those days, some priest or nun seemed to have labeled everything a sin: going steady, strapless evening gowns, even the Beatles. And just to make sure things didn't get too out of hand, on the afternoon before the First Friday of every month all the students were herded into the school chapel for confession. So instead of mystery, Sara was now offered hard and fast rules. Rather than miracles, she found a divinely sanctioned system of reward and punishment. And instead of nurturing young minds toward ethical responsibility, Sara discovered a religion that measured morality by inches and seemed to worship a God who could not accept imperfection in the human condition.

Some of the students were outraged by the audacity of the priest who "banned" the Beatles, even going so far as to lodge a protest with the principal. Sara was more amused than angry. "What else can you expect," she told a friend, "when his two favorites are Bing Crosby and Lawrence Welk?" Sara did ask her mother, however, about the length of her skirt. This time it was her mother who laughed when she replied, "The dear sisters mean well enough, but they live rather sheltered lives. They've never had any children of their own."

Critical Crossroads

Two critical crossroads were soon reached, however, where many of Sara's generation found it difficult to integrate their childhood images of the Christian message with the formulations of the institutional church. The ease or difficulty that adolescents are able to move through these intersections and make the transition from childhood to adult belief will often define their future relationships with the church. These crucial junctures on the spiritual journey are *sexual morality* and *religious authority.*

Sexual Morality

The acceptance of sexuality and its subsequent integration into our personhood is as crucial in the search for spiritual maturity as it is for human identity. Men and women are sown with sexuality; it is part of our bone and marrow. All too often, the church in the past—priests, parents, teachers, and schools—seemed to be on the wrong side of young people's lives. Instead of compassionately supporting a painful struggle toward sexual maturity and accepting the possibility of failure as part of the risk of growth, the institution assumed the role of a punitive parent who seemed to define God exclusively in terms of judge and controller of individual deeds and actions.

Sexual responsibility is a lofty ideal. It can be taught only in a positive way, well-integrated with the whole Christian message, particularly with the ideals of charity and justice. Taken out of the gospel context and expounded in an isolated form as a compilation of don'ts, education in the sixth commandment often entails an inhibiting distortion of truth. The impression conveyed, all too frequently, was that morality was limited to a list of sexual prohibitions outlined against a backdrop of eternal fire.

At the very best, past excesses in the Catholic community's attempts at moral education have provided material for literary efforts from James Joyce's *Portrait of an Artist as a Young Man* to Christopher Durang's *Sister Mary Ignatius Explains It All for You*. At its worst, it has left in its wake many wounded souls who have unfortunately cast aside the entirety of the Catholic faith experience and heritage in rejecting its sometimes extreme strictures about human sexuality. With good reason, then, did the psychiatrist Karl Stern observe in *The Third Revolution:*

> Although I am opposed to our moral relativists who advocate the abolition of "sexual taboos" on the basis of scientific discovery, I have much more sympathy with them than with our Jansenist teachers of morality. The former act often out of natural charity while the latter often give vent to neurotic cruelty under the cloak of moral teaching.

Religious Authority

The second critical task for the adolescent, as well as the adult Catholic, is to resolve the relationship between the institutional church and Jesus. The most simplistic approach, of course, is to deny the need for any ecclesiastical organization at all. As Holden Caulfield once put it in *Catcher in the Rye*, "I like Jesus . . . but I don't care too much for most of the other stuff in the Bible."

This "other stuff in the Bible" presumably means the structures and creedal formulations that evolved in response to the needs of the primitive Christian community. Most Catholics understand that, however romantic an ideal, right from its beginnings the church was never meant to be a totally charismatic "movement" or "happening" of free-floating believers without religious authority or established beliefs.

Catholics also recognize that they share a common bond with other Christians through baptism and acceptance of Jesus as Lord. But at the same time they understand, however vaguely, that they are members of a unique family of faith. The great fountainhead of their identity, as well as their union within this Roman Catholic communion, is the eucharist. And the necessary ministerial source of the eucharist is the "disciples," the bishops of the church in union with the bishop of Rome, the historical successor of St. Peter.

The Problem of Human Beings

It is because of these "disciples of Jesus," however, and the way they understand and exercise their authority, that some Catholics feel tensions. As Edward J. O'Heron aptly describes it, "Crisis of faith tends to revolve not so much around the problem of God but more around the problem of human beings, not so much from the gospel but from the church that proclaims that gospel. In other words, for most people the problem isn't Jesus. The problem is the disciples, that is, the church."[1]

This "problem of human beings" in the church is often the reason why adolescents or young adults are uneasy about the exercise of religious authority. Their tensions occur against a backdrop of major governmental scandals over the past decades, which have resulted in skepticism, even cynicism, about the role of authority, religious as well as political, in a democratic society. This, of course, is not a rationale for the rejection of religious authority, but it may explain, in part, why tensions occur.

Not only is religious authority devalued by the misguided attempts of the "St. Scholastica's" priest to discount the Beatles or the Irish bishop who once banned bikinis, but the image of the church is all too often discredited by the heavy-handed, arbitrary, and excessively legalistic way that people sometimes are treated when attempting to arrange for something as simple as a baptism, a wedding, or a funeral. The annulment process, especially, can be part of a particularly difficult time; people may be wounded unless they are treated with great compassion and sensitivity by church authorities.

A Sense of Perspective

In remembering, it helps for people to reflect upon the story of their adolescence, the times when God seemed particularly close, those moments of great grace and healing, as when David noticed the myriad colors and texture of the pigeon's wings. But for some, it may be equally necessary to focus on how their spiritual journeys have been affected, for better or for worse, by the way sexual morality has been taught within the church and the manner in which its religious authority is exercised. For those who have had bad experiences or have been wounded in either of these areas, it also may be important, in addition to discerning between the human and divine in the church, to deal with the anger and pain that may still be present.

This is not to say that everyone has to leave the church in order to make an adult commitment, but all of us must view the Catholic communion through adult eyes, sifting the wheat from the chaff, the essential from the peripheral. Sister Joan Chittister has eloquently described this aspect of the spiritual journey:

> I started out committed to the "church" and found myself committed only to the Christ. Let those who think the two are the same beware. The problem is to determine where the two merge and where they do not. The "safe" thing is to assume—as we've been taught—that there is no difference. The way of the spirit is to struggle between the two.[2]

REFLECTING

Listed below is a sampling of various religious or church-related activities participated in by many adolescents. Indicate your level of interest or involvement when you were a teenager:

	High Interest	Moderate Interest	Neutral	Moderate Disinterest	Disliked	No Opportunity
Catholic high school	[ ]	[ ]	[ ]	[ ]	[ ]	[ ]
Sunday Liturgy	[ ]	[ ]	[ ]	[ ]	[ ]	[ ]
Receiving Holy Communion	[ ]	[ ]	[ ]	[ ]	[ ]	[ ]
Choir	[ ]	[ ]	[ ]	[ ]	[ ]	[ ]
Prayer/Bible groups	[ ]	[ ]	[ ]	[ ]	[ ]	[ ]
Religious ed classes	[ ]	[ ]	[ ]	[ ]	[ ]	[ ]
Volunteer work	[ ]	[ ]	[ ]	[ ]	[ ]	[ ]
Reading Scripture	[ ]	[ ]	[ ]	[ ]	[ ]	[ ]
Parish teen/youth groups	[ ]	[ ]	[ ]	[ ]	[ ]	[ ]
CYO sports	[ ]	[ ]	[ ]	[ ]	[ ]	[ ]
Serving Mass	[ ]	[ ]	[ ]	[ ]	[ ]	[ ]
Teaching Catechism	[ ]	[ ]	[ ]	[ ]	[ ]	[ ]
Helping out in the rectory or convent	[ ]	[ ]	[ ]	[ ]	[ ]	[ ]
Attending daily Mass	[ ]	[ ]	[ ]	[ ]	[ ]	[ ]

DISCERNING

Pretend you're relaxing with a friend. You're sharing stories of your life and your friend asks the following questions about your spiritual journey. Write your answers for your personal use.

1. Who had the greater influence on the development of your religious values, your father or your mother? How were their values communicated to you?
2. The author of this book says that after the "bouquet of roses" experience "God's loving care seemed very real." What spiritual values or beliefs from your adolescence have remained with you over the years and are still an influence in the present?
3. What critical crossroads did you experience when moving from childhood religious images to adult belief? How did you resolve any conflicts?
4. Did you ever experience a "problem of human beings," a time you were hurt by someone with authority within the church? Have you been able to forgive this person, or are you still angry?
5. When David examined the symmetry of the pigeon feathers, he experienced an epiphany. He saw "that the God who had lavished such craft upon these worthless birds would not destroy his whole creation by refusing to let David live forever." Did you ever have a comparable moment as a teenager when you were intensely aware of God, or some great weight was lifted from your conscience?

Write a letter to someone you love (not necessarily to be mailed) describing a teenage epiphany. Or write a letter to someone within the church with whom you are still angry; share your pain and your desire to forgive.

PRAYING

Jesus, there was so much in my adolescent years
that I took for granted,
so many signs of your love
for which I sometimes forgot to say thanks—
  the parents and family who cared for me,
  starry skies,

my friendships and my happy days,
the love that was there for me,
summer sunsets,
the ways that I have been healed and helped to grow,
the glory of a morning in spring,
the beauty of a bird's wing.
For these and for many other things,
I want to thank you
and ask again
that I may always see your hand in my life and
Never forget to be thankful,
even for your many unnoticed gifts.

SIX

The Road to Corofin: Adult Experiences

And, O my Brethren, O kind and affectionate hearts, O loving friends, should you know anyone whose lot it has been, by writing or by word of mouth, in some degree to help you thus to act; if he has ever told you what you knew about yourselves, or what you did not know; has read to you your wants or feelings, and comforted you by the very reading; has made you feel that there was a higher life than this daily one, and a brighter world than that you see; or encouraged you, or sobered you, or opened a way to the inquiring, or soothed the perplexed; if what he has said or done has ever made you take interest in him, and feel well inclined toward him; remember such a one in time to come though you hear him not, and pray for him, that in all things he may know God's will, and at all times he may be ready to fulfill it.

—John Henry Newman, "The Parting of Friends"[1]

FOCUSING

Thomas Merton's spiritual journey from Marxist undergraduate to contemplative monk has been described in his autobiography, *The Seven Storey Mountain*. Merton was a student at Columbia in the late 1930s, wrestling with the meaning of his life, when he met two men, professors at the university, who were to have a significant influence on his future. One of these instructors, Mark Van Doren, was a professor of English literature; the other, Daniel Walsh, lectured on medieval philosophy. Both men became Merton's friends and confidants; they attracted the young graduate student, not only by their intellectual integrity, but also by their openness, their lack of pretension, and what Merton would later characterize as their "innocence of heart." It was the same quality Merton's friends, then and later, would often see in him.

Strangers overtake us on our journey and we become friends, often because we are neighbors, or professional colleagues, or share some special passion, such as literature, backpacking, or Irish setters. But sometimes our friendship goes beyond a mere commonality of interests. We are attracted to certain people, consciously or unconsciously, because we recognize at a deeper level a likeness, a sharing of values; we identify with them. These friends also become our role models, our mentors, our guides.

Friends and Mentors

This mentoring-friendship relationship happens in a business or ministry setting when one person assumes the role of advisor, teacher, or guide for a colleague. According to Harvard professor Daniel J. Levinson, who has written about this particular relationship, the mentor may act as a *teacher* —the role played by Mark Van Doren and Daniel Walsh in the young Thomas Merton's life—to enhance a friend's skills and intellectual development. The mentor may also serve as a *sponsor* to facilitate advancement; that is, act as a *host* or *guide* into a new professional role or occupational world. The mentor may offer *advice* and *moral support* in time of stress and may also be an *exemplar,* or role model, that the protégé admires and emulates.[2]

It is interesting to note how perfectly Jesus performed the role of mentor in his dealings with his first followers, particularly the apostles, whom he no longer called "servants, . . . but . . . friends" (Jn 15:15), and whom he "began to teach many things" (Mk 6:34). Indeed, the apostles often addressed Jesus as "Teacher," and specifically asked for instruction on many occasions, for example, "Lord, teach us to pray" (Lk 11:1).

The Lord also promised to be their *sponsor*, or advocate, saying, "Very truly, I tell you, if you ask anything of the Father in my name he will give it to you" (Jn 16:23) and, acting as their *guide*, called them to the new role to "fish for people" (Mk 1:17). Jesus assisted his friend Peter with *advice* and *moral support* in a time of great stress, "I tell you, Peter, the cock will not crow this day, until you have denied three times that you know me" (Lk 22:34) . . . "but I have prayed for you that your own faith may not fail; and you, when once you have turned back, strengthen your brothers" (Lk 22:32). Finally, Jesus offered himself as a *model* for them to follow, "For I have set you an example, that you also should do as I have done to you" (Jn 13:15).

Nurturing Our Dream

The most significant role that friend-mentors can play in our lives is to suspend judgment, accept us for who we are, where we are, and not impose their own agenda upon us. They listen to our hopes and fears, but especially support us as we struggle toward the realization of our *dream*. This dream is our vision, our hopes—the sense of possibility for the future that creates excitement and vitality in our lives. It is what Martin Luther King, Jr. meant when he said, "I have a dream." Mentors, in other words, foster our development by believing in us; by sharing and encouraging our dream, however imperfectly it may be defined; by creating a climate of trust, a space, in which we can work toward fulfillment of our future.[3]

So it was that the stranger, when he met the two downcast disciples on the road to Emmaus, restored their hope and gave them back their shattered dream: "Oh how foolish you are and slow of heart to believe. . . . Was it not necessary that the Messiah should suffer these things and then enter into his glory?" (Lk 24:25-26). The stranger departed, but the disciples' hearts were left burning with their memories. Their dream was renewed because "he was talking to us on the road, while he was opening the scriptures to us" (Lk 24:32). The risen Lord is our mentor, too, through the support and encouragement we receive from our friends as we struggle to realize our personal dream.

Thomas Merton's Mentors

At the beginning of our spiritual journey this mentoring role is most often played by our parents or other adult figures, such as a grandparent, an uncle, or an aunt. These significant adults teach us our prayers, point out the baby Jesus in the Christmas crib, or, as in that charming moment in the childhood of St. Thérèse, remind us that our name is "written in heaven." But as we mature, other people's lives intersect our paths and other friends become our mentors. In his best-selling first book, *The Seven Storey Mountain,* Thomas Merton described the role played in his spiritual journey by his friend, Mark Van Doren:

> Mark, I know, is no stranger to the order of grace; but considering his work as teacher merely on the natural level—I can see that Providence was using him as an instrument more directly than he realized. As far as I can see, the influence of Mark's sober and sincere intellect, and his manner of dealing with his subject with perfect honesty and objectivity and without evasions, was remotely preparing my mind to receive the good seed of scholastic philosophy.

One evening in 1939, after Merton had been baptized, he went walking with his other special friend at Columbia, Daniel Walsh. Merton was still troubled about the next step in his life and had sought out Walsh for advice. But Walsh answered his question almost before it was asked, "As soon as we walked out into the cool night, Daniel turned to me and said: 'You know, the first time I met you I thought you had a vocation to the priesthood.'"

The Kindness of Strangers

Often, as in Thomas Merton's conversations with Mark Van Doren and Daniel Walsh, we receive insights about our lives and our directions from friends that we might have otherwise missed. Many of us have also heard a professional colleague or life-long confidant use words or describe situations without any conscious reference to us, words or situations that somehow "hit home," went right to our hearts, like an arrow to a target.

Even a complete stranger can assume, however briefly, the role of a mentor and guide. One night, sharing guard duty during the Persian Gulf War, a middle-aged reservist confided to another soldier his discouragement over his life-long difficulty understanding written words and how somehow he always saw numbers backward. The other soldier recognized the symptoms and casually suggested that the man might be dyslexic. "The light went on," said the reservist later describing the incident. When he returned home he received professional treatment for his learning disability, reshaped his life, and is now fulfilling his dream as a forty-six-year-old college student.[4]

Sara's Adult Journey Begins

In the early fall of 1968, about the time Thomas Merton was packing his flight bag and preparing to leave his monastery on his fateful trip to the Far East and the final chapter of his life's journey in Bangkok, Sara Hughes was beginning her own adult spiritual journey. After graduating from St. Scholastica's, she was entering the state university as a secondary education major. Except for Girl Scout camp, college was Sara's first time away from home, and her adjustment to life in a dorm wasn't easy. Her roommate, a former high school cheerleader, hung out at a college bar several nights a week and didn't have much time for Sara.

So Sara often felt lonely that first semester and sometimes called home more than once a week just to hear her mother's voice. Because of the noise in the dorm, and the constant visiting of her roommate's friends, she found it easier to study in the library. One Friday night, she happened to meet Sister Judy, a campus minister from the Newman Center, and was invited to join the Center's folk group. By second semester, when some of her contemporaries were pledging sororities and others were joining consciousness-raising groups and reading *The Feminine Mystique*, Sara was strumming "Kumbaya" at the Newman Center's weekend liturgies.

Sara plunged into the Center's social service program for the homeless, was elected a member of the parish council, and visitors at Sunday Mass often remarked about the beauty of her voice. She became so active in the campus parish's activities that several times Sister Judy, who had by now become Sara's good friend, wondered aloud about her studies, hinted broadly about priorities, and suggested that there was life beyond the Newman Center. But Sara laughed at the nun's advice and teased that Sister Judy sounded just like her mother.

The Culture of Disbelief

Sara dropped out of the folk group early in her sophomore year, explaining that she needed a break, and soon after her friends began to miss her at Mass. She stopped by the Center once or twice the following spring to tell Sister Judy that she was a dorm resident assistant and was volunteering as a counselor at a campus halfway house for teenage drug addicts. Sara was enthusiastic about the "really caring" people she was meeting in the psychology department, had recently read *The Population Bomb* by Paul Ehrlich, and shared with Sister Judy some concerns about the failure of organized religion to provide answers on world poverty and overpopulation.

Sara also said that she now felt it more meaningful to attend a nondenominational liturgy of poetry and prayer hosted on campus by a popular Unitarian minister. "I need to grow," she told Sister Judy. The nun listened, and then asked softly, "But how do you grow without food, without the eucharist?"

"Sister," said Sara as she got up abruptly to leave, "you just don't understand!" The campus grapevine soon rumored that Sara was spending almost every weekend with a young professor in the psychology department. They exchanged private vows in the presence of their friends by a local waterfall shortly after Sara's graduation.

"He who has ears to hear," scripture tells us, "let him hear." There are times when we are unable or unwilling to accept advice, however sincerely intended. Like the Greeks listening to St. Paul after he had preached in Athens, we are cautious about the consequences and say that "we will hear you again about this" (Acts 17:32). Or the words we hear are so powerful that, like St. Stephen's hearers, we are "stung to the heart" and, figuratively at least, walk away holding our hands to our ears (Acts 7:54, 57). "I still have many things to say to you," Jesus once said to his friends, "but you cannot bear them now" (Jn 16:12).

Mentors in Faith

Many of us also find our mentors among the faithful Christians who have gone before us—those men and women whose past spiritual journeys have somehow touched our lives or that our faith tradition has held up as role models. When I think of faithful Christians, I always remember what happened to me one day on the road to Corofin, in County Clare, Ireland.

When I was teaching at a university some years ago, I used to rent a cottage in a small village in the West of Ireland and take extended summer vacations. My days were spent writing, hiking over the countryside, and photographing the ruins of twelfth-century monasteries. Evenings, I'd head for the pub to hear the local lore, listen to the lilt of the language, and pass myself off as a famous Irish writer to any hapless American tourists looking for local color.

All four of my grandparents had come out of Ireland just before the turn of the century. I was curious about my family history and wondered, most of all, how my forebears had held on to their religious convictions in Penal Times. Penal Times, as every Irishman knows, was that period of time before 1829 when English law repressed Irish Catholicism. The Penal laws, at their worst, banned the Gaelic language, restricted Catholic educational opportunities and professional careers, and proscribed public Catholic worship. Lay Catholics were fined for attending Mass, and priests caught celebrating the forbidden liturgy in some areas were hung.

The Road to Corofin

The great lesson I learned about faithful Christians in the past, whose journeys have touched our own, began one night visiting the local pub. "Do you know where they went to Mass in Penal Times," I asked the pub keeper during a lull in the conversation. "Sure," he answered, "we went to Mass up on the road to Corofin." Then he took a paper napkin and drew a map of the back road to the next town, marking the site of the Mass stone, or outdoor altar, where people worshipped in secret up in the hills during Penal Times.

Early the next morning, at sunup, with camera gear in my backpack and map in hand, I was on the road to Corofin. A couple of miles out of town, up a side path and hidden behind a grove of tall poplar trees, I found it—a gray stone altar with a chiseled Celtic cross. I can't explain exactly what happened next, but at that moment before the stone altar my past and my present suddenly seemed to merge into one. I thought of all the people who had stood there and worshipped at that altar generations before me. My great-great grandparents were surely there, or at a similar altar, under threat of felony and fine. They had passed on the flame of faith for generations yet unborn. For me. "You were bought," scripture reminds us, "with a price" (1 Cor 6:20).

Afterward, the thing I remembered most about that stone altar on the road to Corofin was not only the sacredness of the site, or the wild beauty of the Irish hillside, but the sense of identity in the way the pub keeper had answered my question about the altar's location, "Sure, we went to Mass up on the road to Corofin." Penal Times had ended over a hundred and fifty years earlier, but he spoke as if he had been there, as if it were yesterday. And ever after that moment, I would also say, "We went to Mass up on the road to Corofin."

Hearing Stories

My father, from about the time I was three, used to sit me on his lap each evening after supper and read to me stories of the rich folklore of American history: Patrick Henry declaiming "Give me liberty or give me death!" before the Virginia House of Burgesses, Barbara Fritchie defending her country's flag ("Shoot if you must this old gray head"). But most of all, he related folklore about our famous ancestor, General Phil Sheridan, that flamboyant Civil War cavalry commander who turned a Union rout into a smashing victory with his twenty-mile ride "down from Winchester to save the day."

Even without realizing it, my mind was being prepared to receive the "good seed" that would be nurtured on the road to Corofin and mature as a life-long fascination for the lives of the saints. Not only were the saints members of my family of faith, my Catholic heritage, but in my adult years, after Vatican II, the saints became my role models, the only mentors I could find. They nurtured my dream of what it meant to be an adult believer.

Role Models

From St. Thérèse of Lisieux, for example, I learned to distinguish between the content of my faith and its cultural manifestations and how at the heart of the gospel was the primacy of love. In the life of Newman I discovered the difference between faith and feelings and found a model for the "thoughtful believer." And in the English martyrs—particularly Sir Thomas More, the lawyer; Robert Southwell, the poet; Edmund Campion, the writer; and Margaret Clitherow, the butcher's wife—I discerned the faces of recognizable human beings who chose their own spiritual paths when conformity would have been easier, who dared to put conscience before authority and their informed judgment before the social and religious pressures of their times.

Faith survives, believers survive, Newman insisted, because real holiness is irresistible; it exercises a strange and compelling power over the hearts of men and women. The people in our lives—friends, parents, mentors, patron saints—pass on to us their ideals, nurture us in our journey, encourage us in our dream. It is a generational thing. These holy people transmit the sacred flame of faith far beyond their own time and, in Newman's inspired phrase, "rescue their world for centuries to come."

The Journey of Faith

Flannery O'Connor in her novel *Wise Blood* employs a stunning metaphor for the ambiguity of adult faith. O'Connor describes the tortured spiritual journey of a free-lance Southern evangelist, Hazel Motes, who is trying to escape religious belief, but all the while is obsessed with Jesus. In his madness Motes sees this "wild ragged figure" of Jesus running from tree to tree in the swampy backwoods of his mind, beckoning Motes to follow him "into the dark where he was not sure of his footing, where he might be walking on water and not know it and then suddenly know it and drown."

I like to think that in our journey of faith the risen Christ stands behind our friends and our mentors and, through their words and their lives, beckons to us, calls us out into the dark where, while we may not always be sure of our footing, we are, nonetheless, confident in our direction and sure in our divine companion. As Cyprian of Carthage, a saint who was martyred in A.D. 258, reminds us:

> It is with Christ that we journey and we walk with our steps in his footprints; it is he who is our guide and the burning flame that illumines our path. Pathfinder of Salvation, he draws us toward heaven, toward the Father, and promises success to those who seek him in faith. We shall one day be

that which he is in glory if, by perfect imitation of his example here below, we become not mere Christians, but other Christs.

REFLECTING

Close your eyes for a few minutes and select someone from your adult life who has been a mentor or a person who offered you helpful advice at a critical crossroads. This can be a special friend, a family member, a person met only once; or it may be someone you have never met in person, but would like to have met because of his or her influence on your life, such as a saint, a historical person, or a figure from literature. Close your eyes and think about that person.

Now let that person enter the space in front of your eyes. Notice how he or she walks. Does the person move confidently or hesitantly?

What are the surroundings? Indoors or outdoors? Bright sunshine or cloudy? Describe the room, the furniture, the setting.

What is the shape of the person's body? Does he or she appear comfortable or ill-at-ease? How does the person stand, hold his or her head?

What is your mentor wearing? Visualize the color and cut of his or her clothes. Do they fit? Are they attractive?

Notice that this person is holding something. Ask what it is. How does the person respond to your question? What is it? Do you want it?

Now talk to your mentor. Say what his or her life has meant to you. Thank your mentor for the help, the advice you have received in the past. Describe your own life, your present concerns. Ask your mentor what question about your directions he or she would most like answered. How does your mentor answer? With what words? Talk to this special person.

Finally, ask what questions your mentor has for you. Does your friend want something from you? What is it? Do you hear in the responses your dream, your own lost voices? Is there something you want very much from your mentor?

Talk to your friend and explain your needs. Ask for help once more in your life.

DISCERNING

When the conversation with your mentor has been completed, open your eyes, take your notebook or a piece of paper, and write what you saw. Don't bother about style or spelling. Just write. Be sure to describe what this person's life and advice and support mean to you. Where might you go? What might you do?

If possible, do this exercise with a close friend and share each other's responses.

PRAYING

The reading introducing this chapter contains the last section of the last sermon "The Parting of Friends," which Newman preached upon leaving the Anglican church he loved so dearly. Read it over once more, prayerfully, thoughtfully. As you do, bring to mind one special person who has assisted you in your adult spiritual journey and pray for this person, though you may "hear him not."

Lord, I thank you for all those good people
who have helped me on my journey,
but especially I remember today my good
friend and mentor, ____________________
If she (he) is still on her (his) own journey, I ask
you to assist her (him) as she (he) once assisted me,
if she (he) has come to the end of her (his)
jouney, may you welcome her (him) into Paradise
and may she (he) remember me before your throne.
Lord, thank you for my friend,
and may I mirror your love and mentor the lives of those
other travelers I may meet along the road, those who
call me friend. Amen.

SEVEN

The Sweet Sound of His Voice: Defining Moments

We are slow to master the great truth that Christ is, as it were, walking among us, and by His hand, or eye, or voice, bidding us follow Him. We do not understand that His call is a thing which takes place now. We think it took place in the Apostles day; but we do not believe in it, we do not look out for it in our own case. We have not eyes to see the Lord; far different from the beloved Apostle, who knew Christ even when the rest of the disciples knew Him not. When He stood on the shore after His resurrection, and bade them cast the net into the sea, "that disciple, whom Jesus loved, cried out to Peter, "It is the Lord!"

—John Henry Newman, "Divine Calls"[1]

FOCUSING

Stories of saints and mentors, like family snapshots, are sometimes blurry; the features of individuals may be indistinct. This chapter is about Newman's spiritual teaching, which, unlike some others, stands out in sharp focus against the backdrop of his times and offers men and women of today realistic advice on discerning their directions. In Newman's life, and the choices he encountered, we recognize a human face.

Newman's Journey

Newman, who was born in 1801 and died in 1890, was an Oxford scholar and Anglican Vicar of St. Mary's, the university church. Newman's homilies, published as *Parochial and Plain Sermons*, were best-sellers in the Victorian era and, over 150 years later, are still in print. His friends were many, his personality warm, and people from all over England either wrote or visited Newman for advice and guidance. One visitor described his first meeting with Newman, then in his fifties, this way: "I found him most kind, ever so nice, and full of fun."[2] By every standard Newman's holiness was unique, the spiritual direction he offered practical and down-to-earth.

Newman's sense of his vocation never remained static but underwent a gradual evolution. By 1843, for a number of theological and historical reasons, Newman reached, as he characterized it, the "deathbed" of his Anglican days. He resigned his position at the university, retired to a country retreat, and began writing his seminal theological work, *An Essay on the Development of Christian Doctrine*.

After two years, under a strict regimen of prayer and fasting, Newman decided that his new direction lay within the Roman communion, which he joined in 1845. The following letter, written to his sister, Jemima, suggests the painful human and spiritual price Newman paid reaching this decision. While anxious to be faithful to the call of the Lord, he also worried about hurting former friends and suffering a serious loss of income from declining sales of his books resulting from his choice:

> What in the world am I doing this for (I ask myself this), except that I think I am called to do so? I am making a large income by my sermons. I am, to say the very least, risking this; the chance is that my sermons will have no further sales at all. I have a good name with many; I am deliberately sacrificing it. I have a bad name with more; I am fulfilling all their worst wishes, and giving them their most coveted triumph. I am distressing all I love, unsettling all I have instructed or aided. I am going to those whom I do not know, and of whom I expect very little. I am making myself an outcast, and that at my age. . . . Continually do I pray that He would discover to me if I am under a delusion: What can I do more? What hope have I but in Him? To Whom should I go? Who can do me any good? Who can speak a word of comfort but He? . . . May He tell me, may I listen to Him, if His will is other than I think it to be.[3]

Difficult Decisions

Newman's anxieties did not cease with his entry into the church of Rome. In the years that followed, Newman again faced major questions about the direction of his life. At first he had to decide what religious lifestyle he and his early companions would follow. Should they join the Jesuits, Benedictines, or Redemptorists? After weighing several options, he decided upon the Oratorian rule of life as the most practical for their needs.

Then Newman felt called to undertake a completely new ministry to the poor in the industrial inner city of Birmingham, rather than launch a crusade to convert the English upper class in London, as expected by many members of the Catholic community. Next, he decided to begin a preparatory school for the education of young Catholics. After another period of serious soul-searching he took up temporary residence in Dublin during the 1850s and established the Catholic University of Ireland. Later he became editor of a magazine, *The Rambler*, began a translation of the Bible, and set out to open the first Catholic Center at Oxford University.

Some of Newman's projects failed; others were thrust upon him by the force of circumstances; sometimes his talents were thwarted needlessly by a well-meaning but uninspired hierarchy. But never a person to accept events passively, Newman always attempted to move forward into life, to be faithful to his "kindly light"—conscience—and discern his own pathways. His plans and directions changed many times, so it is clear that he was speaking from his own experience when he wrote, "In a higher world it is otherwise; but here below to live is to change, and to be perfect is to have changed often."

Newman also believed that Jesus is present to us—and as accessible through faith—in post-resurrection times as he was to his friends a few days after the first Easter. In other words, Newman taught that the risen Christ stands just beyond the veil of the present moment and though hidden from our eyes, speaks to us through the circumstances of our lives as he once spoke to Magdalene in the garden, the downhearted disciples on the road to Emmaus, or the apostles across the water.

Divine Calls

The second element in the discernment equation outlined in Chapter One is the "spiritual wisdom of the Christian community." After identifying our life experiences or stories from childhood, adolescence and adulthood, the next step is to validate these insights and intuitions in light of the inherited wisdom and spiritual tradition of our faith community, the church.

Our guide in this process is Newman, who believed that there are some unique situations in all our lives that are specific occasions of the Lord's call and provide an objective way of validating our own insights. He first detailed these special life events in a sermon, "Divine Calls," preached in 1839 during a time when he first faced serious questions about the direction of his own life. He considered this sermon so significant in explaining his pilgrimage of faith that a quarter of a century later, when writing his autobiography, *Apologia Pro Vita Sua*, he included sections of this same sermon. The life events described in this chapter come from Newman's own experiences and the unique insights of his spiritual teaching. The particular names or categories assigned to the events, and the examples used to illustrate them, are my own.

1. **Friendship** is the first of the special circumstances through which we hear God's call. Newman is speaking of friends who are the occasion for a sort of prophetic grace in our lives, friends who give us a deeper insight into the life situation in which we find ourselves.

At Oriel College at Oxford in 1826, for example, Newman met for the first time a brilliant young scholar named Richard Hurrell Froude. Froude soon became one of Newman's closest friends. While Froude shared Newman's spiritual sensitivities, his theological background at the time was much richer than Newman's. Froude was a medievalist and had a sense of the church as a historical fact, which Newman had yet to acquire. They often sat talking in the Oriel College common room or went riding together, and through Froude Newman gradually came to an understanding of the real presence of Christ in the eucharist, an appreciation of the sacramental system, and an awareness of the Christian community as a historical reality.

Curiously, Newman's conversations with Froude, and the effect of their friendship upon his religious development, would find a parallel approximately one hundred years later, one warm September evening in 1931. Two twentieth-century Oxford professors, J.R.R. Tolkein and C. S. Lewis, walked under the beech trees along Addison's Walk and discussed long into the night the person of Christ. Lewis, at the time, was an agnostic and saw Christ merely as a historical figure without any personal relevance to his life. Tolkein, a Catholic and author of *The Hobbit* and *Lord of the Rings*, pointed out that this perception was really a failure of Lewis' imagination and that he should respond to the story of Christ as he would any other heroic myth, but with this difference—that it really *happened*. Lewis later acknowledged that this conversation with Tolkein had much to do with his coming to belief.

Newman's description, in his sermon "Divine Calls," of the way God can call us through our friends could apply to J.R.R. Tolkein as well as to Richard Hurrell Froude:

> We get acquainted with someone whom God employs to bring before us a number of truths which were closed on us before; and we but half understand them, and not half approve of them; and yet God seems to speak in them, and Scripture to confirm them. This is a case which not infrequently occurs, and it involves a call to follow on to know the Lord.

2. The loss of a loved one is another way that the Lord often chooses to speak to us. This can happen either through death or departure. Most of us see death every day on the front pages of our newspaper or on CNN, and we can accept, in the abstract, the inevitability of death, even our own. But the sudden loss of a loved one—a parent, a spouse, a child, a professional colleague, or a close friend—brings its own special call from the Lord. For a fleeting moment our defenses and distractions are forgotten, and we are brought face to face with the meaning, not only of the lives of those we loved, but of our own lives as well. We are forced to confront what is important to us in this world and what is insignificant. And we are offered the opportunity to choose once more the direction we wish our lives to take in the future.

An example: Mary Newman was her brother's youngest sister. She was his favorite and often wrote him laughing, teasing letters. At the end of the Christmas holidays, early in 1828, Mary was taken ill with an acute appendicitis and died quite suddenly. She had just turned 19. Her death was a stunning blow to Newman, and ever afterward, even as an old man, he could never speak of Mary without weeping. But as Newman later explained in his famous *Apologia Pro Vita Sua*, he saw a particular providence in his sister's loss: "The truth is, I was beginning to prefer intellectual excellence to moral; I was drifting in the direction of the Liberalism of the day. I was rudely awakened from my dream . . . by two great blows—illness and bereavement."

A contemporary illustration: Madeleine L'Engle, the author of the best-seller *A Wrinkle in Time,* was married for more than forty years to Hugh Franklin. Franklin was a successful actor and, in addition to the legitimate theater, played the role of Dr. Charles Tyler in the long-running television serial *All My Children.* In her book *Two-Part Invention,* L'Engle movingly describes her husband's losing battle with cancer and tells how, despite Hugh's death—and indeed because of it—she found a new realization of meaning in married love:

> Does a marriage end with the death of one of the partners? In a way, yes. I made my promises to Hugh "till death us do part," and that has happened. But the marriage contract is not the love that builds up over many years, and which never ends. Hugh will always be part of me, go with me wherever I go, and that is good because, despite our faults and flaws and failures, what we gave each other was good. I am who I am because of our years together, freed by his acceptance and love of me.

Then there are the "deaths" we suffer because of the departure of a loved one or the loss of familiar patterns in our lives. These departures are often associated with growth—a son or daughter leaving home for college and saying farewell to friends and family, a recently married couple turning away from the singles scene, a bachelor or a single woman falling in love.

There is also that terrible "death" called loneliness, which comes with the ending of a relationship, whether destructive or life affirming. Here is the way Martha, who is approaching middle age, describes "death," the pain she suffered after a man with whom she felt very close abandoned her for another woman,

> I thought Mark and I had a special relationship. Now I feel like a castoff. There is something wrong with me, something lacking. Something Eileen—I find it hard even to think her name—has that is more attractive. . . .
>
> I thought I was special in his life, as he has been in mine. I believed him when he told me how much I meant to him, how much he loved me. Now I feel elbowed aside, a reject. And I feel stupid for having believed him. I'm angry at myself for letting myself be duped, and I'm angry at Mark for saying he loved me. . . .
>
> Yesterday I was ready to tear up every card from Mark, throw out the stones we had collected together, the shells, the Swedish ivy he had given me, the sweater, everything that reminded me of him. Today, whenever any memory comes up or anything reminds me of him, I have been reaching into the dark painful space in me and repeating, "in the Light of My presence, the dark does not exist."[4]

While the separation this author so movingly describes brings its own sadness, its own death, it also offers its own redemption. Sometimes we learn great wisdom in loving unwisely.

Twelve years have passed since Sara Hughes's marriage at the time of her graduation from college. Her husband, Doug, is in the psychology department of a small New England college, and Sara is a music teacher at a local high school. Their first years together were the happiest Sara had ever known. She was Doug's ideal woman: cheerful, optimistic, willing to take care of herself, and full of spontaneous warmth and affection. Doug was strong, thoughtful, had a sense of humor, and liked music. They worked all week and on the weekends hiked in the Berkshires, attended concerts, visited the Boston museums, and rented a summer cottage on Cape Cod. Once, returning from a skiing trip, Sara and Doug dropped in at the Weston monastery. Doug judged the liturgy "great theater," but Sara wept softly and for sometime afterward her thoughts turned nostalgically toward the faith she had abandoned in college.

As the years passed, the couple's interests—and their relationship—seemed to level off. From time to time they argued. Sara faulted Doug for his lack of ambition in advancing his career and completing his book; Doug complained that Sara spent too much time and too many nights on after-school projects.

Their son, Kevin, was born after eleven years of marriage. Doug hired a young graduate assistant as a live-in baby sitter to help Sara with the child care after she returned to teaching. "I should have seen it coming," Sara later confided to a friend, "but I trusted him—right up to the day he announced he wanted an 'open marriage.'" When Sara ordered the graduate assistant out of her home and refused to go along with Doug's new lifestyle, he packed his things and left.

In the months that followed, Sara put away her wedding pictures and took off her ring. After her divorce, she and Kevin moved to a small town in upper New York State where she obtained a teaching position. It was winter and the house always seemed cold. She took good care of her little boy, but sustained herself with hard-boiled eggs and corn flakes. She hated the king-size bed, and at night lay there, her mind racing over the past and into the future, trying to make some sense out of her life, her despair.

3. Scripture. Dan Wakefield, in his book *Returning*, describes the beginning of his spiritual journey. He experienced a "thirst" for God and then joined a Bible study group at a local church. He soon discovered that the prayerful reading of scripture is not like studying history, but more like holding up a mirror in which persons sometimes see what they are trying to keep hidden even from themselves,

> The first Scripture passage I was assigned to read was from Luke, about the man who cleans his house of demons, and seven worse ones come. I did not have any trouble relating this to "contemporary life." It sounded unnervingly like an allegory about a man who had stopped drinking and so was enjoying much better health, but took up smoking marijuana to "relax," all the while feeling good and even self-righteous about giving up the booze. It was my own story. I realized, with a shock, how I'd been deceiving myself, how much more "housecleaning" I had to do.

Wakefield makes the point that it is all too easy to evade the demands of the gospel and dismiss Christ, narrowly and unfruitfully, as a shadowy historical figure somewhere "back there" in time. Vague statements about his love, his mercy, his compassion for the multitudes, however well intended, do not move our hearts.

But the prayerful reading of scripture puts Jesus before our eyes in the actual events of his life, in his words and work, his gestures and deeds, that "wild ragged figure" beckoning us to follow him off into the dark. This means, as Frederick Buechner has observed, that scripture, the Bible, is ultimately about you and me. Of all the books that the human race has ever written, the Bible "is the one which more than any other—and in more senses than one—also holds us together."[5]

4. Contemporary literature. The book of Numbers relates a curious event that happened during the Israelites wanderings in the desert. They complained bitterly to Moses about their diet; nothing to eat but manna. Moses, in turn, complained to Yahweh, "I am not able to carry this nation by myself alone; the weight is too much for me."

So the Lord instructed Moses to select seventy men from among the elders of Israel, bring them to the meeting tent, and the Spirit of God previously given only to Moses would also come upon the seventy elders who would then share some of Moses' burden. Now it happened that two men, Eldad and Medad, had remained behind in the camp and had not gone to the tent with the others. But the Spirit of Yahweh came upon them also; they began prophesying in the camp. Joshua was scandalized at this prophesying of Eldad and Medad apart from the seventy authoritatively appointed elders and demanded that Moses stop them. But Moses accepted their efforts, refused to silence them, and answered, "Would that all the Lord's people were prophets, and that the Lord would put his spirit upon them!" (Nm 11:1-30).

Sometimes religious people, like Joshua, become so accustomed to seeking God only through "appropriate" channels—through scripture, or spiritual reading—that they become narrow and one-dimensional. They are blind to the lesson of Eldad and Medad: the Spirit of the Lord breathes where it will and is not restricted only to "approved" or "religious" ways of communication.

This is the reason a mature believer must also be aware of the literature, film, and art of the age, not only to learn how other men and women deal with the same dark doubts, the same wild hopes, that we all endure, but also through these events to hear the voice of the Lord. In some way the writer and the artist experience and are able to express the meanings in life, which are as yet at the unconscious level, but will later be explicated by the saints and scholars of the community. How eloquently, for example, does Flannery O'Connor describe the radical ambiguity of faith in the madness of Hazel Motes; how subtly is the existence of God hinted by the "controlled rapture" of John Updike's slate-blue pigeon feathers; how poignantly is the fundamental issue of human existence raised by Hamlet's cry of existential anguish, "To be or not to be, that is the question."[6]

5. Defining moments. Chapter Four opened with a hauntingly descriptive passage from writer Annie Dillard. She recounted a moment from her past, when she was a little girl sitting on the floor, idly playing with her fingers. Suddenly she somehow became aware of life, of time: "Time streamed in full flood beside me on the kitchen floor; time roared raging beside me down its swollen banks; and when I woke I was so startled I fell in."

Similar threshold experiences occur in all our lives, no matter what our age. These are revelatory events; they are somehow bigger than life. God calls us through these happenings. "These moments bring with them an awareness," as John Shea writes in *Stories of Faith*, "that we have a relationship not only with the events themselves but also to the Mystery of life within which they occur."

An illustration: In one of my spiritual journey workshops, a middle-aged man, with tears in his eyes, shared with other members of his group his memories of an event that had happened on a Fourth of July over fifty years before—his seventh birthday. He described a completely happy day—opening presents, blowing out the candles on his cake, watching fireworks with his family. But as he lay in bed that evening, listening to the faraway sounds of a summer's night, he was suddenly overwhelmed with intuitions of his own mortality. For the first, but not the last time in his life he realized that this day and this moment were gone forever. The events of that Fourth of July were symbolic of a basic life meaning; years later he could look back upon the event and say, "That's what it's all about."

Literature and life are filled with these revelatory incidents. Some are universal experiences: a gaggle of geese against an autumn sky, the majesty of a sunrise, a baby sleeping in a crib, the touch of a lover's hand. Other moments have a special meaning only for an individual person, but their memory, like the scent of a delicate perfume, lingers long after. For Newman, it was a moment at sea when the clouds parted and his "kindly light" formed a silver pathway across the darkened waters. For Grant, the priest at a clerical funeral, it was the sudden realization that "the corpse was in better shape than the congregation." For Sara Hughes it was the lyrics of a song.

Sara's Homecoming

After the numbness of her divorce and moving to a new school and its students, Sara had settled into the life of a single mother in a small, upstate New York town. About a year after her arrival, a neighbor invited her to a newly-formed scripture study group at the local Catholic church. Sara felt uncomfortable attending, but her friend needed a companion, and Sara was beginning to think about Kevin's religious upbringing. Deep down, she also felt nostalgic for the faith she had once loved but had abandoned in college.

The study group was small, and Sara, reluctant to talk publicly about religion, remained silent the first few weeks. But the elderly priest seemed a well-intentioned, compassionate man, and Sara began to participate. At home she started to pray again, first with the faintly remembered prayers of her childhood, then more and more in her own words.

One night, at the coffee break, Sara mentioned her earlier visit to the Weston monastery and someone in the group dropped off at her home a recording by the monks at Weston. When Sara put on the record and heard the monks sing,

> Come back to me with all your heart.
> Don't let fear keep us apart.
> Long have I waited for your coming home to me
> and living deeply our new life.[7]

She began to cry. She also felt herself strangely "starving" for the sacraments. The next day Sara knelt beside the priest in the rectory parlor and went to confession for the first time in over fifteen years.

Invitations to Love

Christopher Buckley tells a true story about novelist Graham Greene. Greene, it seems, had heard about the stigmatic priest Padre Pio, whose hands and side would bleed, like the wounds of Christ, while saying Mass. So Greene went to a remote village on a Sunday, entered a back pew of the church during Padre Pio's Mass, and sure enough, the priest's hands began bleeding during the elevation of the host and chalice.

This was too much for Greene. He left Mass, went out to a sidewalk cafe at the edge of town, and ordered a drink. He finished his drink and was getting ready to leave, when he saw a young priest running toward him up the street. The priest told the startled Greene that he had a message from Padre Pio: "Be at peace, God does not ask anything from us that we cannot give Him."[8]

Padre Pio's message to Graham Greene is, in a way, a summary of Newman's spiritual teaching. God never *demands* what is beyond our ability, what we cannot give, but at special moments in our lives—through friendship, loss of a loved one, the reading of scripture or contemporary literature, and threshold events—the Lord *invites* our love and affirms our intuitions about new directions. And our response to these calls? In his sermon "Divine Calls," Newman suggests this:

> Let us beg and pray Him day by day to reveal Himself in our souls more fully, to quicken our senses, to give us sight and hearing, taste and touch of the world to come; so to work within us, that we may sincerely say, "Thou shalt guide me with Thy counsel, and after that recline me in glory. Whom have I in heaven but Thee? And there is none upon earth that I desire in comparison of Thee. My flesh and my heart faileth, but God is the strength of my heart and my portion forever.

REFLECTING

Review your own life for a few moments and for each of the following five headings select a moment or event when God was particularly present to you, whether you realized it at the time or only later. For now, just write a summary phrase or sub-heading in your notebook identifying that moment. An example for "The Loss of Loved One" could be "Leaving home for college and moving away from my family roots for the first time."

1. The Advice of a Friend:
2. The Loss of a Loved One:
   Through Death:
   Through Departure:
3. Scripture:
4. Contemporary Literature (or music, film, or art):
5. A Defining Moment:

DISCERNING

Select what you consider to be the most significant of the above events in terms of your spiritual journey. On a separate sheet, or in your notebook, describe the experience or event in detail. Expand on its particular meaning for you. Include the following:

- When did it happen?
- What were the circumstances?
- Were you alone or with others?
- How was God calling you?
- Did you realize at the time the uniqueness of the event or moment? (If later, when did you begin to appreciate the meaning of the event?)
- What mystery or meaning did the event or happening convey?
- What lesson did you learn?
- How is your present life influenced by that special moment?

If you have the opportunity, share your writing with a close friend or spiritual mentor.

PRAYING

Lord, you gave sight to the blind
  and hearing to the deaf,
Draw close to me and those I hold dear;
  touch our hearts,
  quicken our senses,
  and reveal your loving care for us
  in the special moments of our lives.
May you be the joy of our hearts,
  the strength of our lives,
  and our portion,
  forever.
O that today you would listen to his voice!
Do not harden your hearts.

—Psalm 95:7-8

EIGHT

The First of All Roads, the Last of All Roads: Journey of Faith

The question is not whether the things that happen to you are chance things or God's things because, of course, they are both at once. There is no chance thing through which God cannot speak—even the walk from the house to the garage that you have walked ten thousand times before, even the moments when you cannot believe that there is a God who speaks at all anywhere. He speaks, I believe, and the words he speaks are incarnate in the flesh and blood of our selves and of our own footsore and sacred journeys. We cannot live our lives constantly looking back, listening back, lest we be turned to pillars of longing and regret, but to live without listening at all is to live deaf to the fullness of the music. Sometimes we avoid listening for fear of what we may hear, sometimes for fear that we may hear nothing at all but the empty rattle of our own feet on the pavement. But be not afeard, says Caliban, nor is he the only one to say it. "Be not afraid," says another, "for lo, I am with you always even unto the end of the world." He says he is with us on our journeys, he says he has been with us since each of our journeys began. Listen for him. Listen to the sweet and bitter airs of your present and your past for the sound of him.

—Frederick Buechner, *Listening to Your Life*

FOCUSING

When Bruce Catton was researching his three-volume history of the Civil War, he discovered a letter written by a Union officer, Colonel Strong Vincent, to his wife just before the battle of

Gettysburg. The letter described a summer's evening, the last day of June, 1863, as Vincent watched his brigade march to battle through a rural town somewhere in Pennsylvania.

The regimental flags were unfurled and the young men paraded through the town in step with bands playing. In every doorway teenage girls in white dresses waved flags and cheered. Vincent turned aside from the line of march and watched the flags float by and on down the road. To an aide he confided that there could be worse fates for a man than to die fighting there in Pennsylvania.

Vincent was mortally wounded two days later at Little Round Top, and this was his last letter home. But as he reined in his horse and observed his column marching by, he somehow realized the terrible beauty of the events unfolding before his eyes in that Pennsylvania twilight. For these young women who had been nowhere, and had all their lives before them, as Catton would later describe the scene, that long white road in the moonlight was "the first of all the roads of earth," and for many of the young men marching by "it was the last of all the roads." But for both, young men and women alike, that journey and that moment transcended time and touched the "unutterable mystery" of life.[1]

The first of all the roads; the last of all the roads. Sometimes it is only when we are "jerked out of the ordinary," to borrow a phrase from Thomas Merton, only when we gain a certain distance from our daily patterns and pathways, only then do we achieve a new perspective and see the larger implications of the whole expanse of our life. Not that we necessarily look back in longing and regret, but we review our past interests and present directions, "like the angel of God, discerning good and evil" (2 Sm 14:17). This, after all, is the lesson learned by Galen Rowell and his wife after the canceled photographic assignment, when they had the opportunity to break the bonds of the ordinary and achieve a vision, as fresh and as clear as the dawn of a new day, of hometown architecture, but also of life.

Sacred Pathways

Authors have struggled to find appropriate images for the journey within, for our path to the sacred. In describing the adult journey Daniel Levinson writes of life's "seasons." Gail Sheehy some years ago delineated its "passages," and even Shakespeare speaks of life as if it were a "stage" and men and women "merely players." But even a superficial reading of scripture—the Israelites' wanderings in the desert, for example, the Egyptian and Babylonian captivities, the experiences of Noah, Abraham, Isaac and Sarah—suggests that many of the holy men and women of the Hebrew scriptures lived their lives literally and spiritually "on the road."

> All of these died in faith, without having received the
> promises, but from a distance they saw and greeted them.
> They confessed that they were strangers and foreigners on
> the earth, for people who speak in this way make it clear
> that they are seeking a homeland.
>
> —Hebrews 11:13-14

On the Road

Jesus had "nowhere to lay his head." He was born while his mother was on a journey; early in life became a refugee in a foreign land; and upon reaching maturity was back on the road telling stories. He spoke of other people who had made journeys ("A man was going down from Jerusalem to Jericho. . . "), was often "tired out by his journey," advised his followers "to take nothing for their journey . . . no bread, no bag, no money," ended his earthly life while on a journey to Jerusalem, and was buried far from home in a stranger's grave.

These scriptural allusions, and the clear language of the eleventh chapter of Hebrews that faith is "the assurance of things hoped for, the conviction of things not seen," all reveal the journey theme as the pivotal metaphor in the Judeo-Christian religious tradition. They suggest journey as the central motif not only because we may move spiritually from point "A" to point "B," grow in our prayer life, say, or become more truly accepting of others' foibles and failings, but because journeying to a strange land, being a stranger and a foreigner, a refugee with no friends and family waiting in welcome, is a powerful symbol of what it means to live a life of faith in a secular world.

We are always moving on through the town into the future, seeking our true homeland. The spiritual journey, our life in faith, is the first and most important of all our roads and also the last of all our roads. But this pilgrimage doesn't happen in romantic isolation, like a winter plant growing in a miniature greenhouse on a kitchen windowsill. Our growth is exposed to all the elements, to the killing frosts as well as the renewing sunlight of the circumstances of our lives. So it was that St. Thérèse of Lisieux, experiencing the warmth of her father's love, found it easy to recognize the loving care of her heavenly Father. On the other hand, the life-long scars of Thomas Merton's cold and rejecting mother affected his relationships, for better and for worse, with all the other women in his life.

A Dual Citizenship

The great paradox of our spiritual journey, then, is that we hold two passports, have a dual citizenship. It is not only that we try to live a life of faith contemporaneously with all these other events and circumstances, but that the motivation for this *internal* journey is so radically different from the *external* securities, the high level of comfort held out to us as an ideal by our surrounding culture. Unlike corporate benefit packages that offer the security of the golden parachute and equity participation, or financial planning that helps us save on taxes and promises a comfortable retirement, or psychotherapy that provides a feeling of well-being and emotional security, the life of faith is a summons to a radical insecurity:

> By faith Abraham obeyed when he was called to set out for a place that he was to receive as an inheritance; and he set out, not knowing where he was going (Heb 11:8).

Our spiritual journey is not moving from the unsafe to the safe, from the insecure to the secure, but the other way around. In accepting faith we are called, as Abraham was called, to leave our "home"—all the things we cling to in this life—and begin a journey over which we have no control, never really knowing where we are going. Here is how Newman described it in his sermon "The Ventures of Faith:"

> If then faith be the essence of a Christian life . . . it follows that our duty lies in risking upon Christ's word what we have for what we have not; and doing so in a noble, generous way,

not indeed rashly or lightly, still without knowing accurately what we are doing, not knowing either what we give up, nor again, what we shall gain; uncertain about our reward, uncertain about our extent of sacrifice, in all respects learning, waiting upon Him, trusting in Him to enable us to fulfill our own vows, and so in all respects proceeding without carefulness or anxiety about the future.

False Securities

"Proceeding without carefulness or anxiety about the future"—Newman's ideal. The only problem is that people on a spiritual journey can become so overwhelmed by the risks and the ambiguities that they are tempted to turn aside from their true direction and seek instead the deadening stability of safe paths and secure ways. Scripture reminds us, by stories of their waywardness and wanderings in the desert, how the Israelites turned from the way of the Lord by "an evil heart of unbelief" (Heb 3:12). They became restless and dissatisfied, asked for flesh when the Lord had fed them with manna, fretted over water, murmured against Moses, and sought full stomachs and even the "security" of slavery rather than the unpredictable risk of following the Lord's call to freedom,

> If only we had died by the hand of the Lord in the land of Egypt, when we sat by the fleshpots and ate our fill of bread; for you have brought us out into this wilderness to kill this whole assembly with hunger (Ex 16:3).

Nor is it only the tribes of Israel who sought fleshpots and false securities rather than face the uncertainties of their flight from Egypt. The continuing temptation for believers, even today, is to look for reassurance and ultimate meaning in *external* signs and avoid the risks and ambiguities of the *internal* spiritual journey. Newman noticed, even in his day, that certain groups of believing Christians seemed particularly vulnerable to this temptation.

Sensory Consolations

There are Christians who seem to experience a variety of charismatic graces after accepting the Lord as their Savior—the gift of tears, speaking in tongues, ecstatic feelings of joy, slaying in the Spirit. Newman never saw these sensory consolations as essential to the Christian experience. He was even cautious about encouraging excessive affectivity in religion because he had observed, particularly among the evangelicals of his day, that the constant need for emotional intensity in religious practice can divert some Christians from the interior journey of faith, as if it were not more blessed to believe than to see:

> They will not be contented without some sensible sign and direct evidence that God loves them; some assurance, in which faith has no part, that God has chosen them . . . not considering that whatever be the manifestation promised to Christians by Our Lord, it is not likely to be more sensible and more intelligible than the great sign of His own Resurrection. Yet even that, like the miracle wrought upon Jonah, was in secret, and they who believed without seeing it were more blessed than those who saw.[2]

Another group of Christians who seemed particularly tempted to substitute security for faith were some of Newman's Roman Catholic co-religionists. He was concerned that Catholics could turn aside from a life of faith by relying excessively, for reasons of spiritual security, on certain symbols unique to Catholic belief and practice. There can be idols in our lives that we do not recognize as idols, Esther De Waal has written, because they were once helpful in our spiritual growth, were once good in themselves. "It is the clinging to them when the time is past that prevents us from clinging to God and God alone."[3]

Answers and Absolutes

This desire for security rather than faith within Roman Catholicism seems to occur most often in one of two ways. First, there are those Catholics who substitute secondary religious devotions, such as private revelations, pilgrimages to sites of alleged apparitions, and a highly romanticized piety honoring certain saints, for the primary focus of the spiritual journey—union with Christ in loving service of others. Other Catholics, uncomfortable with the inherent ambiguity of the spiritual journey, seek answers and absolutes by overemphasizing the dogmatic and authoritarian aspects of Catholicism; they act as if the pope were an oracle independent of the church.[4] For example, W. G. Ward, a prominent writer and lay theologian of Newman's day, once announced, quite seriously, that he would like an infallible papal pronouncement delivered daily to his breakfast table with the morning paper.

Even without infallible pronouncements with the morning paper, a journey of faith does, of course, presuppose certain stabilities in life. After all, the purpose of a journey is to arrive at a destination. So for a spiritual sojourner, forging a path to the sacred is not a rationalization for emotional rootlessness. Whatever pathways we may follow, there must always be a sense of continuity with our past, symbolized by our human need to come home, to be at home, to return home. For unless we are "home," how can we answer the door when Christ knocks and asks entrance in the person of the stranger? The parable of the Prodigal Son (Lk 15:11-31) is more than just a story of forgiveness; it also reminds us that we cannot set out on a journey unless we have a stable base from which to leave and to which we can return.[5] So it is with the journey of faith, and so it was with Sara Hughes.

Sara's New Life and Interests

After her move to the small community in upper New York State, Sara's life and interests seemed to settle into a pattern that was new, yet somehow familiar. Although she had never lived in the area before, in many ways she had returned home. She found herself at Mass almost every Sunday and sometimes during the week. She still had her occasional feelings of anger thinking about Doug, but, for the first time in many years, she began to feel comfortable with herself and experience moments of genuine peace.

One day her overworked parish priest asked Sara if she would volunteer to train the folk group and start a liturgy committee. Sara said yes, and remembering her days at the Newman Center, soon discovered that she not only enjoyed this after-hours ministry but was making a genuine contribution to the Sunday liturgies and spiritual life of the parish. In fact, she found her avocation so satisfying that after two years as a volunteer, and with her mother's assurance that she would be happy to look after Kevin, Sara decided to seek professional accreditation in liturgical studies and entered a summer graduate program at the University of Notre Dame.

Graduate school only confirmed her new interests, but she was still unsure of her future. The summer she completed her degree, she answered an ad in the *National Catholic Reporter*, more to test the waters than from any urgent need for change. She was surprised, a few weeks later, to be invited out for an interview and then hired as director of liturgy at St. John's, the suburban Midwest parish. "You either go forward, or you die," Sara explained to her teacher friends. She reasoned that a change for Kevin would probably be easier now rather than when he was in high school.

So Sara moved forward into the future. There were many anchors in her life—faith, family, her son, and her professional identity—but, as for most people, there were also many ambiguities. How do we learn to live with the memories of our mistakes and accept our less-than-perfect lives? How do we make our spiritual life a journey without becoming too safe or comfortable? How do we hold to our values and yet remain open to the possibility of growth and change?

The Ambiguity of Faith

It comes down to this: There will always be an ambiguity about our spiritual journey that is nothing more than the very ambiguity of faith itself. We live a mystery; we believe, but we never really know for sure. To illustrate: Bicycling into town early one evening during one of my summer stays in Ireland, I noticed a curious phenomenon—every field I passed had only one tree right in the middle of the open land.

I had a friend in the area whom I will call Sean. Sean had done very well with business ventures in Dublin and moved back to County Clare, where he now lived as a gentleman farmer on a large estate. So in the pub that evening I asked Sean to explain the single tree in the middle of each field. "The real reason," he confided as he nodded in the direction of the other farmers standing at the bar, "is that those poor fools think the leprechauns and fairies like to dance around trees in the moonlight and if they cut down the last tree, the wee folk will get angry with them and make their cows sick. Did you ever hear anything so stupid in all your life?"

I acknowledged that it did seem pretty foolish, but then reminded Sean that each of the fields on his estate had only one tree. "Well," he said, lifting his pint, "you never really know for sure now, do you?" No, Sean, you never really know. For a journey in faith is, after all, in Newman's words, "risking upon Christ's word what we have for what we have not . . . not knowing either what we give up, nor again what we shall gain."

REFLECTING

Up to this point our method of discerning has moved on two levels simultaneously. First, we have listened to the stories of specific events in our lives, both those that are peculiar to us personally, but those, too, that our religious traditions suggest may be particular carriers of meaning. Then we attempted to "see through" the surface details of these individual occurrences and touch the "unutterable mystery," the hints of transcendence that are both veiled and revealed by these events. Now we will listen to the "sweet and bitter airs" of our past and our present for the sound of God's voice, the meaning that is revealed by the whole sweep of our life's story. It is usually only much later that we are able to look back and realize that what was happening to us was, in some mysterious way, life-giving and liberating.

The following lifeline exercise is designed to tie together the experiences of your childhood, adolescent, and adult spiritual journey—the turning points and blind alleys, successes and failures, dark nights and mountain tops, moments when God seemed very close, times when the Lord was more "present" by his absence—in short, all the experiences that have contributed to you being the spiritual, believing, faith-filled person you are today.

In terms of your career, this exercise is intended to help you think about where you are, where you want to go, and what resources you have for getting there. Here is how Sara would draw her lifeline:

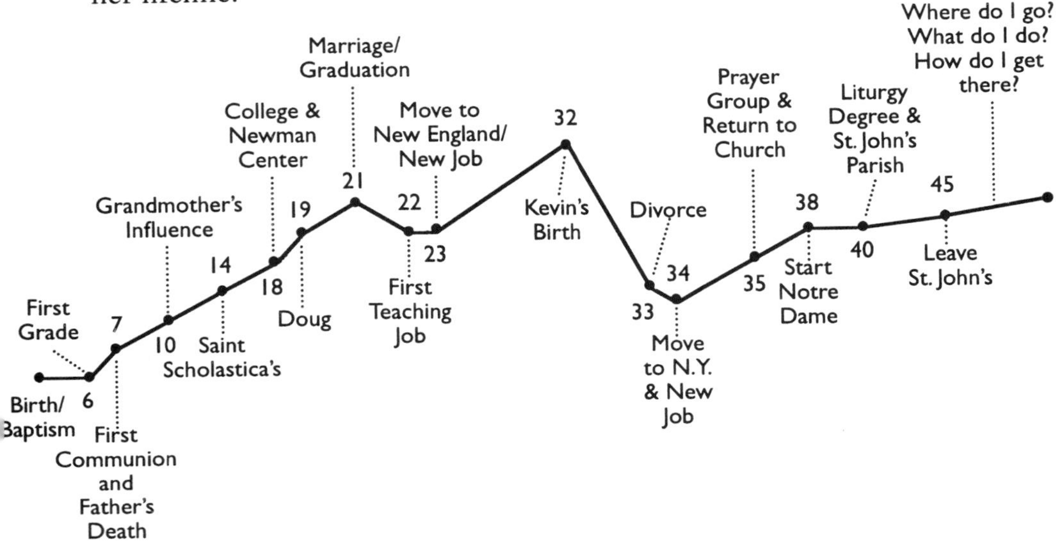

In your notebook or journal, using Sara's lifeline as a model, chart your own journey. Identify the events, the signposts, that have shaped and marked your pathway from past into the present. Vary the direction of the line depending on the impact of these events. Indicate your approximate age at the time these events occurred.

DISCERNING

Using your completed lifeline, place the following symbols along the path:

C	A childhood awakening or awareness of God
AD	An awakening of faith during your adolescent years
A	A significant adult spiritual experience
!	A moment in your life where you could say, "Here was the hand of God"
X	A time you encountered serious obstacles

- O A crucial crossroads of your life or a road not taken
- \+ A point at which you were most completely you, where every thing was "together" in your life
- \- The point of the greatest difficulty you have faced in your life
- ? A time where you see a critical or important decision coming up in the future

Now answer the following questions in your notebook.

1. Have you learned anything about your life or your career path that surprises you?
2. How has the "hand of God" affected the shape of your lifeline?
3. Did you actually make the decisions that affected your life? If not, who did?
4. How might your life have been different without the Lord's loving care?
5. Look at the "unutterable mystery" of the road that stretches before you. What major decisions are coming up in the future. What are your options? What is the greatest obstacle along this road? What is your greatest fear?
6. As you continue along the road, what one practical step are you going to take to move into tomorrow?

PRAYING

As we recall "the first of all the roads of earth," let us also ask the Lord, using the words of Thomas Merton, to remain with us on "the last of all our roads,"

My Lord God, I have no idea where I am going.
I do not see the road ahead of me.
I cannot know for certain where it will end.
Nor do I really know myself,
  and the fact that I think I am following your will
  does not mean that I am actually doing so.
But I believe that the desire to please you
  does in fact please you.
And I hope that I have that desire in all that I am doing.
I hope that I will never do anything apart from that desire.

And I know that if I do this you will lead me by the right
road, though I may know nothing about it.
Therefore I trust you always though I may seem to be lost
and in the shadow of death.
I shall not fear, for you are ever with me,
and you will never leave me to face my perils alone.[6]

NINE

Testing New Directions: Validating Insights

Thank you for taking the time to see me. I will try to be brief and to the point, but let me begin by telling you a little bit about myself:

For the past five years I have been liturgy coordinator for St. John's in Strafford and am a skilled liturgist, church musician, and adult educator. Before joining the St. John's parish ministry team, I was a secondary-school music teacher for approximately seventeen years. My M.A. is in liturgical studies from the University of Notre Dame and my undergraduate degree, from the State University of New York, is in music education.

I have been very successful in parish ministry and liturgy planning, and I have enjoyed my years at St. John's, but now I am seeking to expand my horizons and transfer my skills either to another form of church ministry or even into the private sector.

Over the years I have picked up a lot of expertise in teaching, volunteer recruitment, adult educational administration, program planning, and staff development and training. I am computer literate and am experienced with both Word Perfect and Pagemaker. I have recorded audio cassettes on liturgy planning for the Modern Cassette Library and taught several college-level liturgy workshops for diocesan DREs. My success in reviving the liturgical program at St. John's was recently featured in the *National Catholic Reporter*. For a change of pace, I cross-country ski and play first violin with the Waterford County Community Orchestra.

—Sara Hughes' autobiographical statement

FOCUSING

Wayfarers, whatever the forms of their search, need to cultivate the habit of awareness. Doesn't everyone on a journey notice the signs along the way? Not really. Career consultants and spiritual directors alike see people making major decisions about directions without a real appreciation of their life situations, without attending to the world around them.

All of us have our blind spots. We overlook the obvious and decide our future paths on the basis of intuitions or insights that may or may not be valid. As a result, we miss opportunities that would contribute to our spiritual and human well-being and sometimes choose dead-end directions that result only in failure and frustration. We fail to cultivate the precious habit of awareness, of watching where we are going.

Overlooking the Obvious

Susan Ames, the office manager for a small electronics company, came into a substantial amount of money through an inheritance from an aunt. Susan was very active in the outreach ministry of a small Bible church and for several years had cherished the dream of someday opening a Christian bookstore. Her aunt's bequest made her dream possible.

Soon after settlement of the estate, and encouraged by her minister and members of her prayer group, Susan rented space in a small shopping plaza located in a quiet suburban area. She had scrutinized the catalogues of several major religious book publishers and, using her personal reading tastes and her prayer group experience, ordered a large number of bibles, devotional books, Christian greeting cards, and adult study guides. Next she set up her displays, had a friend design an attractive outdoor sign that proudly proclaimed "Bethany Bookstore," and placed advertisements in newspapers, shopping guides, and local church bulletins.

The store's grand opening, just before Thanksgiving, attracted almost all the members of her congregation and, with holiday shopping and the greeting card demand, business was brisk—until Christmas. In the months that followed, however, customer traffic slowly declined. A few shoppers stopped by, mostly for bibles or seasonal greeting cards, but by late spring business had dropped dramatically. Susan was soon forced to close her doors and suffered a serious financial loss in the failure of her bookstore. The experience left her sadder and perhaps wiser in the marketing of a new business venture.

Susan had a dream, but she made decisions about her new direction without validating her intuitions. She opened the Christian bookstore, but she had never identified a product need, defined her market niche, or profiled her customer base. But it isn't only enthusiastic entrepreneurs and small business owners who may be out of touch with the real world as they plan their new directions. It also happens at the corporate level.

Marketing Diapers in Japan

In the late 1970s Proctor & Gamble had only about a two percent share of the disposable diaper market in Japan. So the company launched a major marketing campaign. Employees dropped off samples at maternity wards and told Japanese mothers to tie a white cloth to their apartment balcony to receive a free supply of Pampers. The promotion worked; sales grew. Proctor & Gamble increased its share of the market from two percent to ten percent almost overnight. Then product sales dropped like a stone.

Proctor & Gamble had overlooked a simple fact: Japanese mothers change their babies' diapers over fourteen times a day—more than twice as often as mothers in America. At the Japanese rate of consumption, the cost of a month's supply of Pampers was too high. Proctor & Gamble never factored usage into their business development equation and, as one executive later described it, they were "out of the ball game."

So, if market research is crucial to the successful introduction of a new product or service, it makes sense that there should also be a similar way in career discernment to validate intuitions and spiritual assumptions about our directions. So far the emphasis of this book has been on personal experience, the way we discern directions in our lives. In earlier chapters we reflected upon our lives at times of different threshold events in childhood, adolescence, and adulthood, the occasions when we saw through the surface realities and discerned meaning behind the mask of the moment. Then we identified those special situations when the Lord seems to speak to us, when we perceive, in faith, his presence in our lives through friendship, the loss of a loved one, scripture, contemporary literature, and defining moments.

Validating Our Insights

The focus of this chapter shifts from discovering our directions by turning *within* to suggest a method of validating our insights from *without*. Self-deception, as Susan Ames learned to her sorrow, is always a distinct possibility. Even friends and spiritual directors, however well-intentioned, sometimes tell us what we want to hear, or what *they* want us to hear, rather than what we *need* to hear. We become victims of our own delusions. That is the reason why scripture advises us, "Beloved, do not believe every spirit, but test the spirits to see whether they are from God; for many false prophets have gone out into the world" (1 John 4:1).

In other words, whether we are considering opening a religious goods store, seeking a new ministry, or just looking to expand our horizons, it makes sense not to decide our directions solely on the basis of hunches. We need to test the reality of our dream first in some objective way—to look before we leap. In the business world this validation process is carried out by information gathering or market research, often through customer surveys or focus groups. I recommend that spiritual wayfarers use an analogous technique in setting their new directions.

Informational Interviewing

This method of defining our directions is variously described as networking, focusing, or informational interviewing. Whatever name we choose to describe the process, after we have traced all the signs of the Lord's presence in our lives, we should contact friends, professional colleagues, and other knowledgeable professionals we may or may not know personally, in order to gather the information we need to help us evaluate our credentials, compare our dreams with reality, define our plans, and test the spirit of our new direction.

But note carefully that the method of informational interviewing I am describing is not a request for a job, not a search for job leads, and not a way to distribute our resume. It is not asking other people to take responsibility for our lives, make our choices, and spell out our new directions. It is seeking a sharing of information and asking for some friendly advice.

Often, when I suggest this approach, the first reaction of clients is negative. They feel that people will be too busy to take the time to visit with them, but they forget that most people, if approached correctly, enjoy giving advice.

Let's look at Sara Hughes's situation to see how the process of informational interviewing works. As Sara Hughes's story opens in the first chapter, she is in a quandary about her new directions after five years as liturgy coordinator at St. John's parish. These have been very successful and mostly happy years in parish ministry, but now things seem to have become routine, Sara's career circle is complete, and she thinks it may be time to move. One friend suggests that she make a retreat and remain where she is; another counsels a complete break and a new direction. Sara isn't sure. Her life has taken some unanticipated turns and twists since marriage, graduation from college, the birth of Kevin, and her divorce. But Sara has remembered the stories, read the signs in her life, and of this she is certain—her passion is music and her love is liturgy.

One day while reading *Successful Woman*, a magazine at her hairdresser's, Sara came across an article on informational interviewing. It seemed to make a lot of sense. Sara took the article home and used some of the letters and formats it suggested to start gathering the information she needed to validate her own insights and to decide her new directions. Sara's autobiographical statement at the opening of this chapter is a good illustration of how someone looking to change direction can tell the story of her career, introduce herself to others, and begin the last phase of the discernment process by conducting "market research" on herself through informal listening sessions or informational interviewing.

Whom Do You Contact?

A good way to start is by asking yourself, "Who would I list if I were asked by a potential employer for references?" In other words, start talking with "warm" contacts first—personal friends and professional acquaintances who know you, who would be sympathetic to your search for a new ministry or direction, and who would give you honest feedback and advice. Start talking to people you know and consider those most open to discussion. That way you can practice describing your skills and career directions and become comfortable with the process.

Sara's list of potential contacts included people who knew and respected her work, such as the editor of the local newspaper, the head of the music department at St. Catherine's College, a trusted DRE from a neighboring parish, and the person to whom she will send her first letter, Dr. Allegra Pavoratti, the diocesan director of liturgy.

To say, "I don't know anybody" or "I don't have many contacts" is an unacceptable evasion. We are social beings and if you give it some thought, you'll be surprised how many potential people you can turn to. The Reflecting section of this chapter contains a generic list of possible sources for informational interviews and a work sheet to draw up your own list of potential contacts. You will likely find that drawing up such a list triggers memories and can assist you in identifying contacts who will help you in defining your goals.

How Do You Cultivate Contacts?

As a first step, I strongly recommend that the career changer write a letter to everyone on his or her list. Again, the purpose of an informational interview is not to ask for job leads; it is to ask for advice. In order that people will not immediately assume that we are asking for job leads, we must take great care to spell out in our letter the "ground rules" for our informational meeting. This written request is so important, that the only time I would not write one would be if I were contacting a dear friend—an ex-roommate, a close professional colleague, a member of a religious community whom I knew very well.

Here is Sara's letter requesting an informational interview:

Dr. Allegra Pavoratti, Director of Liturgy
Diocese of Waterford
918 Church Street
Waterford, IL 54941

Dear Dr. Pavoratti,

For the past five years I have been liturgy coordinator for St. John's parish in Strafford. I am a skilled liturgist, church musician, and adult educator. My M.A. is in liturgical studies from the University of Notre Dame. You may recall our meeting last summer when I presented a workshop on liturgy planning for the diocesan DREs at St. Catherine's College.

I have enjoyed my years at St. John's, have developed an outstanding parish program and achieved all my goals. Now I am considering new directions, and I need to talk to someone with your experience about career opportunities and how a person with my background might best direct her skills either into another ministry or into the private sector.

Please understand that I am not seeking a position with the diocese, nor do I expect you to provide me with employment opportunities. Your practical suggestions and honest appraisal of my plans and possibilities would be far more beneficial to me at the present time. I would appreciate any advice and ideas you may be able to offer.

I shall call your office within a few days with the hope that we can set up a short meeting convenient with your schedule. Thank you for your interest.

Sincerely,
Sara Hughes

Writing

Note carefully how this letter is composed. The first paragraph is really a two-sentence summary of Sara's longer autobiographical sketch that opened the chapter. It situates her in space and time and identifies her to the reader.

The second paragraph explains to Dr. Pavoratti why Sara is writing. She is considering a career change and she needs a favor—some professional advice about new directions and how she could best market herself.

Paragraph three is the "disclaimer" section; it sets up the ground rules for the meeting. Sara makes it clear that she is not writing to ask for a job or for job leads. Although her long-range goal is a new position, all Sara is asking for in this letter is a few minutes of Dr. Pavoratti's time. Her short-range goal is some input to help her validate her intuitions, define her directions, and get a sense of the market for a person with her skills and credentials.

The last paragraph is the "close." Sara says when and how she will contact Dr. Pavoratti. Notice that since Sara is seeking advice and not a job, she does not include her resume; she is not asking for a job, only for advice. Enclosing a resume sends a mixed message.

Telephoning

Keep a copy of your letter. Wait four or five days after mailing it and then follow up with a phone call. Use your letter as a script for the phone call. Here is what Sara said and how she summarized her letter when she phoned Dr. Pavoratti:

> Dr. Pavoratti, my name is Sara Hughes and you may remember that I wrote you a few days ago. . . . As you know, I am the liturgy coordinator at St. John's in Strafford and I am considering some new directions. . . . So you can understand why I am touching base with knowledgeable people in the church community—you might say I am doing some marketing research on my own behalf—and you were the first person who came to mind . . . As I said in my letter, my purpose is not to request a job. Nor do I expect you to provide me with job leads. . . . I just need to sit down with you for a

few minutes of a "listening session"—to tell you a little bit about myself, run some ideas by you about my new directions, and, I hope, profit from your honest feedback.

If you don't reach your contact on the first call, keep phoning. Remember that your contacts have their own priorities, and it may take you some time to talk to them. It is not at all unusual for my executive clients to make eight to nine phone calls before reaching even one potential contact. Keep trying. Your persistence shows you are serious.

The Autobiographical Sketch

Refer back to Sara's personal profile at the opening of this chapter. I suggest that before career-changers start asking others for advice, before they have their first listening session, they draw up a similar autobiographical statement that answers the question, "Tell me something about yourself." This thumbnail sketch, practiced so that it sounds spontaneous and unrehearsed, should be neither so long that it bores our hearers, nor so short or so vague that they are left wondering about who we are and what we do. An autobiographical introduction of about one minute seems just right for most information seekers.

The reason for such a thumbnail background sketch is to ensure that those people we'll be meeting will have an idea of our current professional strengths and objectives. By writing out a personal profile statement beforehand, practicing with a cassette recorder, monitoring our delivery, and committing our biographical sketch to memory, we will not only come across as self-confident and focused in any interview situation, but we provide the other person with a frame of reference. This thumbnail sketch will come in very handy on many different occasions. We can use it when making our case before the personnel board, introducing ourselves to a new bishop or major superior, or actually interviewing for a new position.

The personal profile should cover three areas: 1) where you are coming from; 2) what directions you are considering; and 3) what your credentials are to go there.

Sister Mary Claire, a hospital administrator, is considering a new direction in health-care consulting. Here is how she describes her background at informational interviews:

> I have a fifteen-year career in hospital administration, staff training, and internal consulting. For the last five years I have been administrator of the Geriatrics Medicine Department of St. Mary's Hospital and am now looking to join a consulting firm in the health-care industry.
>
> My Masters degree from Catholic University is in hospital administration, and I also received another graduate degree from the University of Pennsylvania in organizational behavior. I have expertise in institutional analysis and accreditation, program design, hospital staffing, and internal marketing. In addition, I have served on several administrative evaluative teams for other health-care providers, am a skilled presenter, and have published several articles on hospital administration and health-care consulting.

The Informational Interview

The informational interview is a special *focused* conversation between two people. If it is to assist us in validating our intuitions and uncovering the kind of information we need to discern our directions, this informational interview cannot be left to chance. We must control its direction and keep the conversation on track. Here are the basic elements or phases of a typical informational interview:

The Entry Phase

1. Rapport. Start off by establishing a human bond with the person with whom you are speaking. Something in the room will suggest a commonality, an opener for your conversation, for example, children's pictures, the view out the window, a desk ornament. Then say, "Thank you for taking the time to see me. I'll try to be brief and to the point ."

2. Disclaimer. Let the person know, up front, what the meeting is about. Since most people expect you to ask for a job, even though you have already said that is not your purpose, you must explain your motives again. Define just why you are there: "First, I want to make it clear why I am here. As I said in my letter, I am not looking for a position with your organization; I don't expect you to have a job for me. At the present time I am more interested in hearing your suggestions and ideas about how I can best begin defining my directions."

3. Rationale. After stating that you are not seeking a job, explain why you are there: You might say: "I am doing some marketing research. You see, I am in the process of making some major decisions about the direction of my life, and it is important to me that I have enough input—information—to direct me to valid choices. That is why I am talking to significant people in the community such as yourself."

4. Personal Profile. At this point you use your thumbnail sketch to tell your listener where you are coming from, what general direction you are headed, and your basic credentials and skills. Introduce your autobiographical sketch by saying something like this: "Let me begin by telling you a little bit about myself. . . . "

5. Transition. Conclude the entry phase with a short phrase that serves as a lead to the body or main part of the informational interview: "I guess my first question is pretty straightforward. . . ."

The Body of the Interview

The major portion of the interview is, of course, a dialogue between the two participants. It cannot be written out beforehand or scripted as tightly as the entry phase. Just remember to include these two elements in your dialogue:

1. Topics. These carry the conversation along and help the other person to talk. Don't use all of these suggested topics, perhaps two or three at the most. These conversation pieces are only suggestions. Introduce subjects you feel most comfortable in discussing or through which you'll receive the most information. Adapt them to the chemistry of the moment:

- *Compatibility*

Are my ministerial or professional objectives realistic in terms of today's market?

What specific ministries do you see me fitting into?

How would you rate my credentials?

Do my career goals match my qualifications?

How do I best communicate my objectives to professionals like yourself?

■ *Personalization*

How did you first enter this career field?

What made you choose this direction?

How has your own professional life developed?

What are your greatest satisfactions and what do you like the least about your career?

■ *Employment Outlook*

How do you see the present employment possibilities in this field?

What skills do employers seem to seek most?

With my credentials, what kind of a salary should I be seeking?

■ *Possible Directions*

If you were in my shoes, with the background and experience I've described, how would you go about marketing yourself?

To whom would you talk?

What other directions or career options would you consider?

■ *Trends*

How do you read the present career climate in this profession/ministry?

What are the long-term trends?

What changes are anticipated or expected?

How does the local (or regional) experience compare with the national scene?

2. Stories. At the same time that you are discussing the above topics, weave into the fabric of your conversation anecdotes or accomplishment stories that illustrate your professional skills.

While many people know how to dress for success, and have well-rehearsed answers to tough questions, few are skilled at marketing themselves using storytelling techniques.

Well-prepared career stories should flow naturally in the give-and-take of the interview. With a little practice, stories illustrating your abilities can be used to brighten any informational interview and, at the same time, become a powerful technique for self-marketing. We can't be shy about this. We can't wait for the world to beat a path to our door. If we want a particular path or direction, we can't hide our talents under a bushel basket. We must love ourselves enough, believe in ourselves enough, to market our skills to others. Telling accomplishment stories is a powerful way to do this.

To illustrate: Sister Joan Paul, who is considering a career in college administration, is in an informational interview with the president of a small Catholic women's college. In the course of their conversation, the president indicates that the recruitment and retention of superior faculty is one of her prime objectives. Sister responds with this story about one of her past successes:

> I share a similar concern. For example, after I was selected chairperson of the English Department at Visitation Academy I not only upgraded the curriculum, but I made the recruitment of outstanding faculty my top priority. As a result of my efforts, I accelerated the Middle States accreditation process and produced the largest number of Merit Scholars in the school's history.

By telling stories during an informational interview, you may capture a professional colleague's attention, clothe the bare bones of your credentials with flesh and blood, illustrate your talents more graphically, turn a bare recitation of facts into a narrative spotlighting your career successes, and make yourself a memorable person.

The Exit

1. Wrap-Up. "Well, you have answered all of my questions. Thank you very much for your time (patience, courtesy, insights, etc.). . . . I really appreciate your help. May I contact you again if something comes up in the future?"

2. Referrals. "Can you suggest anyone else that I could talk to?" As a modest goal, try to uncover the names of two other contacts from every informational interview. This is the way, after all, to build a network. If the chemistry of the interview feels "right," also ask the interviewer if you can use his or her name as an introduction to these other persons.

3. Resume. Bring your resume with you in case the interviewer asks for it.

4. Thank-you note. Send a brief, handwritten note telling the interviewer how much you enjoyed the meeting, how much you genuinely appreciated his or her help, and how you hope to "touch base" again in the future to let him or her know how your career search is developing.

You still may wonder why anyone would consent to helping another in this process. That's not too unusual. I once had a Russian lawyer, just off the plane from St. Petersburg, as a client. He too was very puzzled about the whole process of informational interviewing. So one day he asked me, "But why should people talk to me?"

If we approach people for listening sessions as outlined above a good percentage of them will take the time to talk with us. People cooperate for all sorts of reasons, among them altruism. Many men and women, if they have the time, are genuinely willing to help. They consider it professional and courteous. Another is that we appeal to people's need to nurture. Many are flattered that you think enough of them to seek their guidance. We are asking for advice, not a job, and advice is free. One executive even explained that it was a good way for him to hone his own interviewing skills and assess talent in the marketplace, an opportunity that usually presents itself only when a position is open.

But mostly, I believe people will talk with us because the Judeo-Christian ethic is alive in our culture. As scripture has it:

> But the stranger that dwelleth with you
> shall be unto to you as one born among you,
> and thou shalt love him as thyself;
> for you were strangers in the land of Egypt:
> I am the Lord your God.
>
> —Leviticus 19:34 (KJV)

REFLECTING

Step 1

As we said earlier, before beginning informational interviews or actively interviewing for new professional opportunities, it helps to focus on our career directions by scripting a brief answer to the standard question, "Tell me something about yourself." Think about your career up to this point and, using as models Sara's autobiographical statement at the beginning of this chapter and Sister Mary Claire's personal profile on page 126 write in your notebook a thumbnail sketch of your own career. Include these three elements: where you have been, where you are going, and what your credentials are to go there.

Practice saying your autobiographical sketch aloud. Record it on a cassette to hear the sound of your own voice. What sounds effective in your statement? What needs to be improved? Use this format to describe your career to a few friends for some honest feedback. Finally, memorize your basic autobiographical statement and then adapt it to different interviewing situations. You will come through to others as a focused, competent, self-assured professional.

Step 2

The following generic list of potential contacts may assist you in identifying people within your community who will help you in defining your goals. Take a few minutes to read through the list. As sources of information occur to you, jot their names in your notebook.

Look up the addresses of your contacts, draw up a mailing list and, after following the outline in the next exercise, write these contacts a letter. Do not enclose your resume.

Potential Contacts for Informational Interviews

- Family and friends
- Social or community contacts
- Parish or church contacts
- Lawyers, financial members
- Professional associaton
- Counselors, therapists

- Professional colleagues
- Religious mentors or spiritual directors
- Graduate school professors
- Exercise or other affinity-group members
- College alumni association members
- Former classmates
- Ex-roommates
- Theologians or writers
- Doctors, dentists, other professional contacts
- Workshop presenters
- Clergy and religious
- Leaders in civic or community organizations
- Placement or human resource professionals
- Diocesan directors
- Parents of former students
- Civic organization members
- Corporate executives
- Librarians
- Former teachers
- Neighbors
- People I once helped along the way

Step 3

Using Sara Hughes' letter to Dr. Pavoratti as a model, write in your own words a sample letter asking a colleague or professional contact for an informational interview. Remember to include these four elements in your letter:

1. A short summary of your autobiographical sketch that introduces and identifies you to your reader.
2. An explanation of why you are writing; that is, that you are considering new directions, doing some "market research" on your career, and need some good professional advice.
3. A clarification that you are not writing to ask for a job or for job leads, but rather are requesting a few minutes of your reader's time for some honest advice to help you define your directions and get a sense of the market for someone with your skills and credentials.
4. A closing that tells, in general terms, when you will call to set up a short meeting.

DISCERNING

Keep notes on each of your interviews. After you have "tested the spirit" and conducted informational interviews, go back to your list and check to see if there are any consistent patterns to the feedback you are receiving. Then evaluate your interviews with these questions in mind:

How many people did I attempt to contact?

With how many contacts did I actually conduct face-to-face interviews?

What was the average length of time for each of these interviews?

On the average, how many referrals did I receive from each interview?

How did I present myself to these people? Directed and focused? A competent professional? Unsure of myself?

Which was the best interview? Why?

Which was the least successful interview? Why?

Did I identify any possible future mentors?

What was the most significant piece of information I received?

Was there a convergence in the feedback I heard? Any common themes?

Taking the interviews as a whole, were my earlier intuitions concerning my directions validated or invalidated?

If validated, what is my next step?

If not, what new directions should I begin exploring?

PRAYING

God has created me to do him some definite service;
He has committed some work to me
    which he has not committed to another.
Therefore I will trust him.
Whatever, wherever I am, I can never be thrown away.
If I am in sickness, my sickness may serve him;
    in perplexity, my perplexity may serve him;
    if I am in sorrow, my sorrow may serve him.

He does nothing in vain. He knows what he is about.
He may take away my friends.
He may throw me among strangers.
He may make me feel desolate,
    make my spirits sink,
    hide my future from me—
    still he knows what he is about.

—John Henry Newman

EPILOGUE

Sara Hughes began her informational interviews by talking to six or seven of her immediate circle of social and professional contacts, including the DRE of a neighboring parish, a newspaper editor, and Allegra Pavoratti, the diocesan director of liturgy. Because of mail delays, telephone tag, and scheduling, Sara took approximately three weeks to complete these interviews, but the feedback she received was sympathetic and almost unanimous: 1) she should seek a change, and 2) her direction obviously should be either music or liturgy.

From these first interviews Sara was referred to nine other people in her community, none of whom she had met before. Allegra Pavoratti suggested that she speak with Dr. Martin Anderson, a dean of the local community college. Sara felt that this was a particularly productive interview and that Dr. Anderson had been impressed with her credentials. But she was still surprised when he called her back a few weeks later to share some information he had picked up at a Chamber of Commerce luncheon: St. Odif's, a Lutheran college in a neighboring community, had recently received a substantial endowment to develop an ecumenical liturgy program in its religious studies department and was initiating a search for a director of this program.

Dr. Anderson suggested Sara contact a dean at the Lutheran college and said to use his name. Sara was the first applicant, and the search process took more than three months. She had four interviews with the faculty committee and was one of five finalists, before finally being selected as the first director of St. Odif Colleges's new ecumenical liturgy program.

NOTES

ONE: Remembering

1. David Lonsdale, S. J., *Listening to the Music of the Spirit* (Notre Dame, IN: Ave Maria Press, 1993), pp. 63-64.

2. John Henry Newman, "Christ Manifested in Remembrance," *Parochial and Plain Sermons, IV* (London: Longmans, Green & Co., 1896), p. 261.

TWO: Career Paths and Work Addictions

1. Bill Peatman, "The Day I Got a Life," *National Catholic Reporter,* December 2, 1994, p. 25.

2. Steven Berglas, Ph.D., "Are You a Candidate for Burnout?" *National Business Employment Weekly,* October 1-7, 1993, p. 27.

3. Stanford Sherman, "Leaders Learn to Heed the Voice Within," *Fortune,* August 22, 1994, pp. 92-93.

4. Francine Dempsey,C.S.J., "Holding Gifts of Fortune in an Open Hand," *National Catholic Reporter,* March 3, 1990, p. 2.

5. Diane Fassel, Ph.D., *Working Ourselves to Death* (New York: Harper Collins Publishers, 1990), p. 116.

6. *Ibid.*, p. 81.

7. Marsha Sinetar, *Do What You Love, the Money Will Follow* (Mahwah, NJ: Paulist Press, 1987), p. 150.

8. Dempsey, p. 2.

THREE: All the Day Idle

1. *Thérèse of Lisieux, Autobiography of a Saint* trans. Ronald Knox (London: Harvill Press, 1958), pp. 255-56.

2. Douglas B. Richardson, "Stop Procrastinating," *National Business Employment Weekly*, August 21-27, 1994, p. 12.

3. Richardson, p. 14.

FOUR: Falling into Time

1. Andrew Greeley, "Because of the Stories," *The New York Times Magazine* July 10, 1994, p. 40.

2. Richard Bode, *First You Have to Row a Little Boat* (New York: Warner Books, Inc., 1993), pp. 201-2.

FIVE: Not Even a Sparrow

1. Edward J. O'Heron, "Don't Lose Faith in Dissent," *U.S. Catholic,* February 1995, p. 23.

2. Joan Chittister, O.S.B., "Today I Saw the Gospel," in *Winds of Change* (Kansas City, MO: Sheed & Ward, 1986), p. 5.

SIX: The Road to Corofin

1. Daniel M. O'Connell, S.J., "The Parting of Friends," *Favorite Newman Sermons* (Milwaukee: The Bruce Publishing Company, 1932), p. 403.

2. Daniel J. Levinson, *The Seasons of a Man's Life* (New York: Alfred A. Knopf, 1978), pp. 97-99.

3. Levinson, p. 91.

4. Sally Pollak, "For Whom Football Is No War," *Philadelphia Inquirer*, Sept. 24, 1994, pp. C1-C2.

SEVEN: The Sweet Sound of His Voice

1. John Henry Newman, "Divine Calls," *Parochial and Plain Sermons,* vol.8 (London: Longmans, Green & Co., 1896), p. 24.

2. Meriol Trevor, *Newman, Light in Winter* (Garden City: Doubleday and Company, Inc., 1963), p. 60.

3. John Henry Newman, *An Essay on the Development of Christian Doctrine* (Garden City: Doubleday Image Books, 1960), p. 63.

4. Francis B. Rothluebber, *Nobody Owns Me* (San Diego: Lura Media, 1994), pp. 106, 107, 108.

5. Frederick Buechner, *The Clown in the Belfry* (New York: Harper Collins, 1992), p. 44.

6. Newman praises the value of secular literature in several places in his writings. One example, among many, is "Literature: A Lecture in the School of Philosophy and Letters" in John Henry Newman, *The Idea of a University* (Garden City: Doubleday Image, 1959), pp. 263-83.

7. *Hosea.* Text and Music by Gregory Norbet, O.S.B. © 1972. The Benedictine Foundation of the State of Vermont, Inc.

8. Christopher Buckley, "God and Man at the Yale Club," in *Once a Catholic,* ed. Peter Occhiogrosso (Boston: Houghton Mifflin Company, 1987), pp. 245-46.

EIGHT: The First of All Roads, the Last of All Roads

1. Bruce Catton, *Glory Road* (Garden City: Doubleday & Company, Inc., 1952), p. 267.
2. John Henry Newman, "The Gospel Sign Addressed to Faith," *Parochial and Plain Sermons*, VI, (London: Longmans & Co., 1891), pp. 108-09.
3. Esther de Waal, "Rootedness or Journeying?" *The Way* (July 1992), p. 202.
4. Charles Stephen Dessain, ed., *The Letters and Diaries of John Henry Newman*, XXV, (London: Thomas Nelson and Sons, 1961), p. 299.
5. Esther de Waal, p. 200.
6. Thomas Merton, *Thoughts in Solitude* (New York: Farrar, Strauss and Giroux, 1976), p. 83.